Thank You.

Blest You

J. B. Sanders

Truth In Life

Learning How To Deal With Life And Its Blows

Johnnie B. Sanders, Jr.

authorHOUSE®

AuthorHouse™
1663 Liberty Drive, Suite 200
Bloomington, IN 47403
www.authorhouse.com
Phone: 1-800-839-8640

First published by AuthorHouse 8/27/2007

ISBN: 978-1-4343-1520-5 (e)
ISBN: 978-1-4343-1519-9 (sc)

Library of Congress Control Number: 2007905543

Printed in the United States of America
Bloomington, Indiana

This book is printed on acid-free paper.

Book Edited by:
Crenshaw & Clay Publishing, L.L.C.
www.crenshawclaypub.com
P.O. Box 701602
Dallas, TX 75370

Acknowledgments

First and foremost, I want to thank my Lord and Personal Savior, Jesus Christ for loving me and showing me how to love. Thank you Lord for giving me life and the inspiration to write these words of transcripts for the growth of your people. Secondly, I would like to thank my anointed and loving wife for her immeasurable support. My heart felt thanks and love also goes to the Sanders family, the Winters family, the Faison family, and the Ross family.

A special thank you goes to my pastor, Bishop T.D. Jakes, First Lady Serita Jakes, their family and the Potter's House family. A special thank you goes to Pastor Rita Twiggs for your dynamic teaching, which I have learned to meditate on day and night. I thank you all for your love, generosity and support over the past 10 years of me being a member of such an anointed church and a loving body of believers.

May the Lord continue to use us and bless us in a mighty way to change the world!

Table of Contents

Introduction

In today's world of hustle and bustle, get to the top, stay on top, look at me, see me, I need it now mentality, has caused a warped cycle of what life is really about. We were not put here on this earth to put each other down. We were not designed to care less about the person standing next to us. You have heard the saying, "what goes around, comes around" or "you reap what you sow." These are very true statements and if you are not careful, the actions that you disburse in the atmosphere, whether it is good or not so good will come back to you. This return unto you will return in some form or fashion that you may or may not be ready for. This cycle of life is a perpetual enigma that has to follow the law that has been implemented by God. From a biblical perspective, we call this element and formula, "Seed time and harvest". You will look forward to seedtime and harvest when you know that you have planted what you want to reap. However, life will present to you challenges that you were not expecting.

The Truth in Life is written to give people hope in their hurt. The stories and the people are real. Most of the names have been changed to protect their privacy. The Lord has laid the stories of pain, heartache, disappointments and physical disability on my heart to write in this format. The over all idea of the messages through out this book is to let others know that they can make it where they are. You will not stay in that place; your past has been redeemed by a predestined future. The questions in life will be explored throughout these passages.

The cycle of life is a mystery within itself. We are born into this world, with no control of it of our own. We are born in a state of sin. Everything about this life, we have to learn and sharpen over time. You may be born with the gift of singing, but you have to practice your gift and allow your gift to grow inside of you. You may have a strong athletic gene that is inserted in you at the child conceiving stage, but it does not reach its highest peak until you practice your gift. We grow up in our culture and we learn different religious concepts, but the power of God draws us into His spiritual acceptance. We live a life of being single and deal with the ups and downs of being lonely, sad, happy, dating, going to plays with friends, dining with your girlfriends or alone. Some of us receive a mate from God and our life is devoted and commissioned to love that person and care for the one who has been given to us as a gift. We gravitate to the Word of God and join a religious institution of our choice. We gather together to gain knowledge, hope, healing, peace and love with our brothers and sisters from the man or woman of God. We do all that we can to do the right thing and to be in our Father's will, but something uniquely happens. This unexplainable thing called life comes in and detours your present existence into a world wind of stress, strain, struggle and uncertainty.

In its simplest form, life can be explained with our thoughts that makes since to us. We can say that the "devil is busy" or "God is testing me", but we don't know the reason why God allows life to intervene in our plans of direction. The bible declares in Isaiah 55:8 "For My thoughts are not your thoughts, neither are your ways My ways, saith the Lord." Our Father and our God formed us with a plan and a purpose in our lives and we do not know the story as we travel along this journey, but there is an expected end by God. He knows what we shall become and what we are specifically designed to do at this day and time. With this being said, how are we going to handle life's issues? When situations in our life come up that are abnormally different than what we are used to, what are we going to do?

In an effort to be transparent with a life-challenging situation, I would like to share a story. It was getting close to the holiday season with family, fun, fellowship, and plenty of food for the eating. Diets were being thrown to the side and napkins were being used by the roles. There is joy in the air and seasonal music playing all around. My family and friends are enjoying one another and we are gearing up for the festive holidays approaching. A really close friend of mine and his wife are having their first child in the season. Everyone is excited because the delivery day is drawing near and we are all buying gifts for the newborn baby and they are painting the baby's room. The couple knew that they would be having a boy because they had the doctor tell them from the ultrasound examination. We received the call that his wife was ready to deliver the baby and off to the hospital several of us went. Everyone's emotions were high and we were praying and singing in the waiting room. The father finally comes out with enthusiasm to say that the baby and my friends' wife are fine. Everyone is happy and hugging and giving high fives to one another. The baby was a healthy 6lbs and 3 ounces and was just as cute as a button. Later on that evening, my friend received a phone call that his mother just passed away. I received the phone call and immediately thought, "You have to be kidding me". His mother was here on earth, just long enough to see this child come into the world, only to vacate this world a few hours later. There was no warning to prepare any of us for this. My friend was holding his newborn baby boy on one hand and weeping over the news of his mother's passing away on the other.

How do you prepare for that? How do you deal with this type of situation? My answer is always Jesus. He is the answer and the way to deal with any and every situation. My friend was emotionally upset and rightfully so. He had questions of why would God do this now? How can He allow them to have so much joy in the morning hours and so much pain that same night? This was a tough situation for me as a minister and counseling was definitely a strain because I was so close to the family. However, Jesus is the answer and He always makes a way out of no way. When I opened my mouth, He gave me the words to say. When I opened my heart, He gave me the things to do. With the Lord's help and guidance, I was able to provide help in a hurtful time in our lives. My friend and his family are doing ok, considering the circumstance. However, it was a process in dealing with the hurt and mourning of his mother's death. The pain did not just go away. The questions did not stop coming up, but the peace of God that passes all understanding, continues to comfort us all.

Your peace of mind is a weapon against the enemy. Life's issues are opportunities to rob us of our peace. In spite of your circumstances, you have the spiritual authority to proclaim peace into your life. The obstacles in life will confront you and you must make a decision. The enemy does not always create a specific incidence, but he will capitalize on the opportunity to steer you into the wrong direction when given the chance. The key is to listen to the small voice on the inside of you, that training in which you have been taught, that guidance that has been instilled in you from parents and friends. When you know where your help comes from, you will refuse to listen to the influence of other voices that are unfamiliar to your teachings. After an established relationship with God, you will come to a place where walking with God will sanction you to fear no evil.

God's anointing on your life comes with a grave price. The children of God, whom He shall anoint for His service and influence, are prepared in a special program to withstand the evil tactics of the devil. The devil will throw obstacles and temptations at you, but life will bring to you hatred from people you help. Life will bring disappointments and thievery from close friends and relatives. The very people that you help, trust, and love may turn around and cause you the most pain. Some of these things that we must face are test that are designed to strengthen you, prepare you, and develop you for the greater elevation from the Lord. The transparency of reading the Word of God is a dichotomy between the will of God and God's purpose for your life.

We are designed to fulfill our purpose in God. This book is a divine tool that has been given to you in love. This book is about life and you will receive love within the readings of the pages. If you are unsure of how to love someone or love yourself, this manual will teach you how to develop love. If you are in tune with love and loving relationships, this will be a refresher course for you. You will identify with the valley lows and prepare yourself to handle the obstacles as you journey to the mountain top experiences. It is very important that you know and realize that you will not stay in that unpleasant situation. You don't have to panic when faced with barriers, but you must prepare, plan and position yourself to enter into that prepared place for you. With every breath that you breathe, allow yourself to worship God. Jehovah Shalom has designed us to worship Him and trust Him, in spirit and in truth. Hold onto God's unchanging hand.

Truth in Life

Chapter 1

Love, Understanding how to Communicate

Genesis 22:2

Then God said, "Take your son, your only son, Isaac, whom you love, and go to the region of Moriah. Sacrifice him there as a burnt offering on one of the mountains I will tell you about."

In today's society, the word love and its meaning has been distorted by the media, music, movies, videos and even some churches. It's unfortunate that this topic has become complicated because it is a very simple element in human nature. We all want it, we all desire it, but we front as if it's not needed and can do without it. I don't care if you are the wealthiest person on this planet or if you're in prison, on welfare, in gangs or rappers who are trying to be "hard" for your homies and fans: you secretly desire to have true love in your life. The world is in search of true love, true friendship, and true acceptance from someone. Oh yes, that's why we are so consumed with the hearts of so many people. We do our best to portray the "right" image to others because we want our look to be of good reputation. This image brings acceptance to those we're trying to gain love and acceptance from in our lives. Being loved and accepted is a great thing. The bible says in Ephesians 1:6, "that we are accepted in the beloved." In relationships, we have to learn how to love. Knowing how to love someone doesn't just happen. There is a spark and chemistry that captivates two individuals, attracts them to one another. There are certain things that draws' you into loving someone and then there are responses that has to be identified and learned by spouses, or mates and couples in order to have a long, lasting, and successful relationship. People do not have to separate or get a divorce, in marriage, if they just take the time to learn how to love one another. In so many marriages today, couples come to the conclusion that we just grew apart. In reality, as one partner grows or gradually advances in life, they fail to include there spouse or mate. He or she fails to give the other an update of where they are and where they are going. It is very vital to keep love and communication in your marriage, we must keep love alive by putting forth the effort to learn how to love and communicate this love to our mate.

In learning how to love our mate or spouse, we need to use positive "Words of Affirmation." I looked up the word affirmation in the Webster dictionary and it states that this word means to declare positively; to assert; to ratify and confirm. People appreciate words that speak well of them. Most couples need wonderful words of acceptance and compliments of satisfaction. We love knowing that we have done something or have said something that meets our mate's approval. Giving small, mere brief words that express that you are pleased with something I did or do builds up your mate or spouse. Our earthly relationships are very important to God. In fact, God essentially said that we must express our love for HIM by loving others, and that is especially crucial for our mates. In 1 John 4:20, it states, "If you do not love your brother whom you see daily, and you say you love ME, whom you have not seen, you are a liar." In order to express our love to God, we must learn how to love one another without walking in envy or strife. We must have love that endures and covers with silence sometimes, as well as verbal. We must learn to love with an agape love. A love of God, which has been shed abroad in our hearts by the Holy Spirit, and HIS love abide in us freely and richly. We must intentionally learn how to treat one another and receive love from one another. Love is an action word and it doesn't just happen. Yes, you're in love with that person, but they do not know it or feel it until you actively take the time to tell them and show them. Oh I hear some of you saying, "She should know it by now. I married her didn't I"? Or, "he should know it by now; I cook and clean up behind him, right"? Those are good steps and necessary when showing communication. However, just like a car, we all need a little fine-tuning every now and then. Let me ask you a question, when was the last time you took her to a movie? When was the last time you rubbed her neck, or her back, and her feet? When was the last time you said that you really appreciate all the hard work that he has done? When was the last time did you just welcomed him home with a big hug and kiss and did not give him a honey do list? These are simple questions and are not extravagant, but we fail to stop and acknowledge the simple small things in our relationships. In the book of Song of Solomon 2:15, the bible reads, "take us the foxes, the little foxes that spoil the vines: for our vines have tender grapes." Now to help you understand what this means and what was taking place here, I will give a little bible lesson. King Solomon has a vineyard in the country of the Shulamites. There was a particular Shulamite woman who worked the vineyard with her brothers. King Solomon would visit the vineyards from time to time and he noticed this tanned and beautiful lady in the vineyards. She was tanned because of the beaming of the sun, as the time of longevity bronzed her skin as she worked in the vineyards. There were other women working there, but the Shulamite woman was the fairest of them all. King Solomon noticed her and wins her heart and eventually takes her to the palace in Jerusalem as his bride. The bible verse is somewhat of a precautionary measure that we should keep the things and people who are dear to us safe from anything or anyone who could harm them or the relationship. When you have a budding love and a precious heart, it's not the large, most obvious things that damage your relationship. It's the subtle, inconspicuous distraction that draws you away into a place that could jeopardize your marriage. We cannot live defensively, but we must seek God for wisdom and direction in every area of our lives.

Wisdom

As we pray for wisdom and as we affirm our loved one. We need to continue with an outward expression of love. We should do and show our love one with taking out "Quality Time." Quality Time is giving your mate, wife, sister, Mother, Father, brother, spouse, or whomever your undivided attention. This builds familiarity, trust and commitment. In the book of Psalms 13:5, it reads "But I trust in your unfailing love; my heart rejoices in your salvation." You must firsts have a relationship with the Lord, in order to learn how to really trust. Many individuals become deeply hurt when they put their trust into someone whom they should not trust. Sometimes we don't see the warning signs because we have not learned how to trust or whom we should trust from the master teacher, Jesus. Trust is very important in relationships and should not be taken for granted nor should it be taken lightly. Doing things together and being together strengthens closeness. Being in the same room, house, office or car does not mean closeness. However, being together should be time of intimate communication. He and she should seek into one another for the intimate details of love that the Lord has whispered to you. Our Father will show you who you should be with, but we sometimes decides to choose someone that we thank is the right partner for us. But when we listen to the Holy Spirit, and we begin to spend quality time with that person that makes us smile, makes our heart skip a beat, makes the gray clouds and the rainy days feel like a refreshing waterfall. That is the kind of intimacy that I am referring to. The quality of the conversations should have words of empathy for the other person. The two people should be sharing their experiences, thoughts, feelings, and desires without any difficulty or barriers. When you are truly trying to experience love, those secrets and past experiences should not stop you from being as intimate with your heart as possible. The quality time that you share with that person should allow you the freedom to talk and share everything about you. The good, the bad, and the not so good are apart of you. All that you have experienced in life has shaped, and molded you into the person you are today. Please don't deprive yourself of experiencing pure love by not sharing your life, your hurt and heart. A loving man, by nature, wants to be more intimate with you and he will want to protect you, nurture you, and love you the way you deserve to be loved. Your encouraging words and intimate moments would make me tread upon serpents and scorpions and thrash the neck of the enemy. When the enemy would come up against us, I would go back to my word that I have meditated on day and night and I would take my shield of faith and quench the fiery darts of the enemy. You see my friends, you have to speak back to the devil and let him know that greater is HE who is in us than he who is in the world. Developing that strong foundation of quality time and intimate conversations is important, and it prepares us to be able to withstand the wiles of the devil.

Giving

With love and communication, a natural occurrence happens that should be expected. I have been blessed with the spirit of giving. For me personally, I love to give and share with others. Giving comes easy for me, so when developing this relationship of love with my mate, relatives, friends, and colleagues, I usually show them love by giving them gifts. I have never tried to buy my way into anything because I believe that is a false act and just like the house that was built on sand, the relationship won't last. The Christian's gifts to God should not be bribes to obtain His favor, but grateful responses to what He has done in our lives. God is the giver of every good and perfect gift (Matt 7:11; James 1:5, 17). We are to give (Luke 6:30, 38), "for God loves a cheerful giver" (2 Corinthians 9:7). Giving itself can be thought of as a gift from God: "Having...gifts...let us use them: he who gives, with liberality" (Romans 12:6, 8). In the physical realm of gifts to one another, expresses to your mate or spouse that you were thinking of them or remembered them. The amount of money or if no money at all was involved does not matter.

There was this couple in Minnesota that I was friends with in my days as a salesman, by the name of George and Beverly. George was an excellent sales man and his job caused him to travel out of town three nights out of the week. Well, George was in New York on a business trip and George bought his wife a beautiful dress from Saks Fifth Ave. Sales were doing well and George knew that Beverly would absolutely love this dress. The dress was made by a famous designer, so it was reasonably priced over two thousand dollars and George was excited about his purchase. George passed by a Hallmark store and he decided to purchase a nice card to go along with the dress. The card was a very nice card, but George felt it need to say more from his heart. So he wrote in the card, "to Beverly, in the mist of traveling all over the country, I stopped for a moment to say that you are always here with me in my heart; Love George". George ships the package to Beverly over night, but his sales meeting was canceled and he caught the next flight out in the morning. George arrived home the next morning just as the FedEx man was leaving he opened the door and went to the bedroom and called out to Beverly, “Honey I’m Home”. He noticed that Beverly was not moving towards him and she was sitting on the edge of the bed weeping. George asked her, what was wrong, did something happen, was she ok? George scanned the room and he noticed that the gift had arrived and the dress was still in the box, unwrapped. He walks over to Beverly and kneels down to her and slightly raises her chin. He asked again, “baby, what’s wrong?” Beverly was holding the card as teardrops fell on the hand written words of George and she whispers to him and says, “I Love You So Much for remembering me while you were away”. As we have all heard, and it is true, that it is the thought that matters. Georges’ simple thought of not just purchasing a gift, but also taking the time to share from his heart words of affirmation to Beverly, caused her to receive a piece of Georges’ heart. Couples give each other all kinds of gifts. From clothes, jewelry, shoes, hats, bikes, cars, to their favorite foods.

Rings

As a young lad, I remember when my father gave my mother a new set of wedding rings for Christmas. At that time, they both had a gold, thin band as wedding rings. The truth of the matter is my father and mother did not have a nest egg of money in their youthful years. My father was a construction worker and my mother was attending Southern University as a nursing student. They were in love and my father did the best with what he had at that time. We all were sitting around the Christmas tree opening gifts and my father said to my mother, "Open this one honey". When she opened the box, her mouth flew open, her eyes began to water and then she covered her mouth. She looked at my father and grabbed and hugged him with such joy and passion. She did not even bother to look at my siblings and me for about thirty minutes. She kept saying thank you to my dad and we wanted to see, but she had such tears of joy and the smile on my dad's face was priceless. The gift my father gave her was a beautiful diamond ring. The ring was shiny and sparkling with many colors as she held it up. It was a wonderful time and my mother treasured her ring and would not be caught dead without it.

As I became older I wanted to find out the significant meaning of wedding rings. Looking at my mothers respect and care of her ring, there was a strong curiosity for me. There are several important meanings of the wedding ring. Many people believe that the roundness of the ring represents eternity. There is no beginning, nor is there an ending. Therefore, the wearing of a wedding ring symbolizes a union that is to last forever. It is a wonderful gift that is a union between the husband and his wife. It is also a spiritual covenant agreement with the Lord. An old folks' belief of the wedding ring was that a vein or nerve ran directly from the "Ring Finger" of the left hand to the heart. This was very profound for me, even as a teenager. I thought back on that Christmas morning and I remembered the expressions on my parents' faces and as I mentioned before, they were priceless.

Servant

The feeling and response of the heart should display love in the form of the "Actions of a Servant." Responding with a servant's love is to be humble, and take care of someone else's needs. To go back to my parents' experience, my dad put his own needs on the side in order to purchase the rings. Your mate or spouse will do things that they know you would like and appreciate simply because they love you. You should have a heart to serve and please your spouse because you want to express your love for them. To serve someone is to show respect and honor. In John 12:26, Jesus says, "If anyone serves ME, let him follow ME; and where I AM, there MY servant will be also. If anyone serves ME, him, MY father will honor." With simple small acts of serving, you will greatly make your spouse appreciate you more. Husbands can serve your wives in the capacity of cooking, cleaning the house, and taking care of the kids. Wives can serve your husbands by preparing his food, assisting with washing the car and ironing his shirts. God finds honor in your serving and smiles blessings on your marriage.

In early history, each wandering family or tribe relied on its members to supply its needs. As society became more complex, tribes began to settle into specific areas with larger groups. As this happened, people became more dependent on each other. Skills and occupations became more and more specialized. Farms and other businesses grew in size, demanding servants and hired hands.

As society developed, the skills needed began to change. The early wandering Hebrew herdsmen lived in tents of animal skins, which they could prepare by themselves. When they started to move into houses in towns, they needed a wider variety of skilled laborers. They needed builders, carpenters, bricklayers, and many other trades and occupations to build and maintain the houses. The more civilized society had a wider variety of needs. It demanded occupations and trades, which could fill its clothing needs, provide health care, education, and other needed products and services. Ultimately, it needed skilled rulers and government officials to govern and maintain order. Yes, society has changed from those primitive times, but the need for people to come together and serve one another is still needed.

In our quest for true and long lasting relationships, we need to further our moments of intimacy of love with the expression of the human touch. It is a blessing to be in a relationship with positive, warm, and comforting touch. It is amazing what just one touch will achieve in a relationship. The touch of your mate is an emotional expression of communicating love. Holding your mate's hand, hugging them just to show them love, is a form of expression that energizes the heart and we really can not explain why. Yes, the act of lovemaking is very important, but you must show other ways of expressing the love of the physical touch. You should rub your mate's neck, or massage their back or lotion and rub their feet. To touch your mate's body is to touch into their soul. Take the time to have intimate moments and touch your mate and communicate with them because you want to know what they really enjoy and what their intimate desires are. You want to know how to communicate in a loving way to them, so you can have a stronger, loving relationship. I am not saying this is a cure for all, or a complete fix of all problems in your relationship. Different issues will arrive, but your bond with your mate will be strong enough to go through whatever storm that comes your way.

Let me give you some biblical examples of how a simple touch can change your environment and your outcome in a situation. In Genesis 3:2, it reads, "but God did say, you must not eat fruit from the tree that is in the middle of the garden, and you must not touch it, or you will die." The Lord gave two important instructions. One, do not eat the fruit from the tree and two; if you touch it you will die. Exodus 19:11-12, the Lord was speaking to Moses, "Be careful that you do not go up the mountain or touch the foot of it. Whoever touches the mountain shall surely be put to death." 1 Chronicles 16:22 "Do not touch my anointed ones; do my prophets no harm." The story of the woman with the issue of blood was another powerful touch. Matthew 9:20-21, "And, behold, a woman, which was diseased with an issue of blood twelve years, came behind [Him], and touched the hem of His garment: For she said within herself, If I may but touch His garment, I shall be whole." My point is the touch is a powerful expression and can be properly used or improperly used or unwelcome. In these examples I have shown you the good and the bad uses of the touch. Please be aware of your touch. The more that we comprehend and realize the difference; the more we can fight against abuse. Let's work on our relationships with love and tender loving care. We all want and need to be loved. It is an easy cycle if you allow yourself to feel.

The power of love and marriage is a sacred Christian agreement and is not just a contract between a man and a woman. The relationship of a husband and wife should be compared to the relationship to Christ and HIS church, Ephesians 5:25, “Husbands, love your wives, even as Christ also loved the church, and gave himself for it.”

In my humble opinion, marriage is the highest and most blessed of relationships. Love in relationships and marriages are expressed in all forms. Give love whole-heartedly and God shall bless you and your mate.

Father I pray that you will increase the love amongst your people and that friendships, relationships, and marriages become stronger within your power. Holy Ghost, I pray for expedient delivery from bondage, from low self-esteem and I pray that there will be an out breaking of love and devotion towards one another.

In Jesus name we pray, Amen!

Chapter 2

Life

Deuteronomy 30:15
See, I set before you today life and prosperity, death and destruction.

All of us have times when unpleasant life circumstances come along and knock the wind right out of us, and we feel a sense of failure, shame, defeat, rejection and a ton of emotions that have been conjured up within ourselves.

Life all by itself will bring obstacles that we have to overcome. Yes, Satan will throw things at us from time to time, but everything is not the devil. Satan or his imps do not orchestrate all hurts and disappointments. We as believers sometimes give the devil way too much credit when trials and tribulations come. The bible says that we shall have trials and tribulation in this lifetime. Let's think about this for a minute, Our Father, Jehovah, Our Lord and Personal Savior is omnipresent. God is everywhere at all times and he knows where we are and what we are going through. However, Satan is one being, which has to get permission from Jesus to even temp us. (Job) Satan does not have the power or ability to be everywhere at the same time. His power is very limited to our risen savior, Jesus, who went to the grave and defeated death and removed the sting of the enemy and received all power in HIS hand. Satan can threaten us no longer once we accept the Lord as our Personal Savior.

So with that knowledge, how do you handle losing your spouse? How do you handle losing your health, your job, your best friend, wrongful imprisonment, not getting that stage play part or record deal? It is human nature to ask God "why". Why did this happen to me? Why did he die? Why did she leave? Why am I overlooked again for that promotion? Why does my father always have to work? Why? Why? Why? We must seek the Lord to get direction, to gain peace, to have our lives saturated with God's presence. When you have these emotions don't run from them, deal with them. Be honest with yourself and be honest with God. So many times we try to help God out by saying "oh, God did not see it or he's to busy to deal with my issue". We convince ourselves that God does not want us to be honest with HIM about our lives.

We think that God will be upset with us if we told HIM how we really felt. Trust me, God knows how you feel. He knows every thought before we can think it. Jesus wants us to be honest with HIM, with ourselves, with family and friends and anyone else who come in our lives to play a significant part. In Psalm 51:6, it reads "Behold, thou dost desire truth in the innermost being, and in the hidden part, thou wilt make me know wisdom".

When life hits us with blows of non-expectancy, we must learn not to lean on our own understanding, but trust and remember ALL Things work together for the good to them who are the called according to HIS purpose. So understand that spiritual warfare will come as well as the obstacles of life. We have to prepare ourselves for both because the Lord, who is in control, will develop us to what HE shall have us to be. While we are going through our issue, we become weary, we loose sight of what the Lord has shown us previously. Life begins to hit us at every angle and our faith begins to waiver and our self-esteem begins to lower and we start to have self-doubt within ourselves. Now whether you are a spiritual veteran or a baby Christian in this battle, we must remember how to go to God in prayer and we need to go to God's word for answers. God's word will remind you of whom you are to HIM. The word of God will remind you of your self-worth in this life. The word of God will remind you that HE has come to give you life more abundantly. John 10:10, the thief comes only to steal, and kill, and destroy: I came that they might have life, and might have it abundantly. We have to remind ourselves that we are the "head and not the tail". If it is God's will, we may have what we say. I am not talking about naming it and claiming it. That is too shallow for me. Did God speak that name into you to claim it? If not, shut it down, fix it up and be quiet! Do not miss your blessing and deliverance by chasing after someone else's victory. Do not allow the enemy to trick you into thinking that someone else has your blessing and it should have been you, hold up and hold on. You better bridle your thoughts and bridle your tongue before you set yourself up for a fall. God does not make mistakes, we do! We will make grave mistakes when we're unsure of ourselves or not sure of why this something happened to us.

I remember working very diligently and affectively on the job and there were several rumors or talks going around about me getting this up coming promotion. The position was a very prestigious position within the company and it was going to be an increase in my salary into the six-figure range. However, there were a few people that were promoted all around me.

Most of them I trained and some of them talked about me getting promoted, but it did not happen. Months went by and nothing happened for me. The Holy Spirit shared with me that increase was coming my way seven months ago, but I did not get promoted. Several VP's of the company interviewed me for several positions in an executive role and all the interviews went well, so I thought. However, I never was promoted. Well in that eighth month I received a phone call from an outside source, inquiring about me to render my service to them. I was a little surprised because this was someone out of the blue that presented an opportunity for me that was right up my alley and I already was doing it on a lower level. You better believe I seized the opportunity and I have been operating very well since then. That opportunity did not just happen for me. There were certain spiritual and natural preparations that I had moved on prior to this point. The Lord will send blessings your way, but are you prepared for it? The Lord has a unique way of showing us the end of the blessing, but does not show us how we're going to get there. Nor does HE show us what we're going to have to go through to obtain this blessing. The point that I'm trying to make is don't give up! Don't listen to the enemy when he tells you that you're a fool for believing in all that spiritual stuff. Don't listen to him when he says that

Christ doesn't love you. Your family and friends don't love you. You just need to kill yourself. The devil is a liar and I want you to know that I Love You! You're not in this fight alone!

Homeless

There was this young lady by the name of Lisa. Lisa's parents didn't want her when she was born, so immediately after birth they placed her in foster care. Lisa was shuffled around from place to place, from home to home and hoped and prayed that one day her biological parents would return and love her. Unfortunately, in Lisa's story, this never happened. As Lisa experienced different families along the way, she was always trying to adjust. She even had to deal with being molested by a family member. After years of feeling less fortunate, Lisa developed a disturbing attitude and she lashed out at the world by attempting suicide. She was found and treated at a nearby hospital. Lisa did not have insurance, so after the doctors did all they could do for her and she was stable, she was released from the hospital. Today she lives on the streets, sleeps in doorways and eats from garbage cans.

Sadly, her story is not unique to us. I'm sure that if you think about it, you have seen a "Lisa" on the neighborhood street corner or under the bridge. The Lisa's of this world does not feel loved anymore. Those fairy tales in her mind has been stomped down and away or they are just a faded memory. Lisa did not ask to be brought into this world, but her life has been a hard and dreadful life. Too many of life's blows have hit Lisa without any support, or love, or teaching and has caused Lisa to not know her significance. Lisa does not know her purpose in life. This is why the church body has to have solid foundation and leadership. The Lisa's of the world need to be able to come freely to the Pastors and churches for support, for direction, for love, for mending the broken pieces and shattered dreams. Many wonderful children of the Lord have wrestled with inferiority, poor self-image and lack of self-respect. What do we do as saints who have arrived? Instead of loving them we label them. We put them into this category and compartmentalize them and we treat them as if they're not worthy of our "good mornings" or "God Bless You's". Instead of caring for them and loving them and allowing them to grow into the word of God, we criticize them and talk about their hair, their clothes, their shoes, their different vocabulary, and their personality that doesn't conform to yours. What should we do? We should open our hearts and minds to love on them. We were not always in the position that we're in and we needed time and help to get an understanding of what the Lord would have us to do. The truth be told, most of us are still trying to figure out what is our purpose in life. Please remember that love is much more than shaking hands or giving hugs in church. That's great and it is a part of fellowshipping, however, it takes time to develop and grow. So be gracious. Remember, that tough exterior that you walk around with is just a cover up from your real and true self. As you grow into the knowledge and emotion of loving others, look for new ways to reach out, encourage, and show hurting people you care. Why? Because Jesus said in Matthew 25:40, '"...inasmuch as you did it to one of the least of these...you did it unto Me." And that's reason enough!

Humbled

Having a humbled heart and a grateful attitude is priceless and it is a spiritual trait that is honorable unto the Lord. Have you ever worked extremely hard on a project and presented to your leader and they took your work and nothing was said to you about the finished product? Yes, that has happen to me. On the other hand, have you as a leader or someone who was in a position to help someone in need and they receive your help and do not show or share that grateful gratitude to you. They just take that meal and go on their merry way. They just take the monetary gift and leave without even an utter of thanks. Let's see how Jesus handled gratitude in HIS experienced with the saints at that time. In Luke 17, the Lord was passing through Samaria and Galilee and HE entered into this village. There were ten lepers that saw Jesus when he entered and they stood a distance from Jesus, but they yelled out to HIM. They didn't just yell out to any man, they knew exactly who this particular man was and believed that HE could heal them. Imagine ten screaming voices yelling out to Jesus "help us Jesus, help us". I guarantee you that when they saw HIM they didn't drag their feet, or waste time, or make excuses about why they could not get Jesus' attention. The bible says they raised their voices and asked Jesus to have mercy upon them. Now when Jesus saw them, HE didn't go to them. HE just spoke to them and told them to go and show themselves to the priest. (Luke 17:14) As they walked to the priest, all lepers were healed at the same time, at that same moment. I need to point that out because it was not as if one was healed halfway to the priest, and four others were healed once they arrived at the presence of the priest and the remaining five were healed the next day. All ten of the lepers were healed at the same time, but only one of the healed lepers returned to Jesus to give him praise and glory for the miraculous healing that has taken place in his life. The man was rejoicing and praised Jesus with a loud praise and fell upon Jesus feet with his face. Now Jesus was appreciative that this man came to him with a heart of gratitude. However, Jesus asked this simple question, "Were there not ten cleansed? But where are the nine?" HE was not down playing this one man's rejoicing, Jesus is the master teacher and HE took this moment to show us the heart of gratitude. The expression from your heart should be an expression of you giving back when you have been blessed. Showing gratitude is coming back to say thank you to the person or persons whom helped you and who made whatever you were going through all better.

Gratitude for us is a learned discipline. It is not a natural expression or instinctive emotion that we just freely give. It's the same as when you receive a piece of candy as a child and you don't say thank you and your mother say to you, "where are your manners?" and you reflect back for a moment and say thank you. You practice this in similar settings when you have been blessed to receive gifts. You realize this even the more in kingdom blessings and we all should realize that the gifts from God, which we receive daily, we neither deserve them nor are we entitled to God's blessings. HIS blessings are freely given to us and we cannot earn them, we cannot buy them, we cannot bribe the Lord thy God. At our best, we are mere graced recipients of all we have in our life and all that the Lord has made us. We must show humility. Again, this is a learned attribute that we acknowledge God and HIS blessings and we submit to HIS will and realize that we cannot get through this life without HIM and we cannot do anything alone.

Heavenly Father, as you teach us your will through this life, I pray that we become astounding students that never let you down. I pray that as life changes over time, that you continue to prepare us for the journey that you have set before us, before the creation of the world. Dear Lord, we know that there is a higher calling upon our lives. As we stretch forward to explore all that life has in store for us, we shall keep in mind that our steps are ordered by the Lord. So when we run into obstacles, we can remember that all things work together for good to them that love God, to them who are the called, according to His purpose. We love you Lord and we thank you. Amen!

Chapter 3

Lilies

Song of Solomon 2:16
My beloved is mine, and I am his: he feedeth among the lilies.

One of my favorite flowers is the Calla Lilies. I first came into the knowledge of Calla Lilies when my father bought my mother a bouquet of White Star Burst Calla Lilies for Mother's Day. My mother smiled with a smile of sunshine. Not only were these flowers beautiful, but also they had a fragrance that just exuded the room. My father gave my mother her flowers and said, "Happy Mother's to my Queen". I was able to see first hand how to treat a lady from my father. He was not the most charismatic man, but he was true. My father was true to himself and to mother. He did not try to become this man that he was not. He did not try to be this man that he saw on television, who was suave or debonair. Yes, he liked Sammy Davis Jr., Mr. Sam Cook, and Sidney Portier. My father even liked Frank Sinatra, John Wayne, and Mr. Blue Suede Shoes himself, Elvis Presley. All these men and more my father admired, but he knew who he was and he operated in the best man that he knew, himself.

It's easy for us at times to pretend or emulate someone else. It's good to emulate someone who is positive and who has achieved great accomplishments in life. When I was in high school, I would pattern my study habits after my teacher, Mr. Grady. Mr. Grady was a very astute man. He was a very smart man and he carried himself with class all the time. Mr. Grady would walk in the classroom before the bell would ring, lay his brief case on the desk and systematically pull out today's class assignments. He would separate the test papers in one area as he began to erase the chalkboard. He was very cordial to all the students and when the bell would ring, Mr. Grady would greet the class with, "good morning class and how are we doing today". Now don't get me wrong, he was very kind, but he was no push over. He had a way of commanding with respect without raising his voice. Mr. Grady had rules for the class that he went over with the entire class at the beginning of the semester. His rules were strict, firm, but fair. As a student, you knew when you had messed up in class before Mr. Grady addressed you. Most of the students followed the rules and most of the students wanted to do well in his class. Mr. Grady had a way of making you feel that you were important and you could achieve great accomplishments in life, not just in his class. He would talk to us about the class subject, but he would broaden our minds by challenging us to think beyond those walls. He would say, "Think past these walls, think past the walls of your mind, your home, your family and reach past the stars of life". Well for some reason Mr. Grady had a certain interest in my well-being. At that time I was a B student and I thought I was doing very well. Mr. Grady asked me to come and see him after my seventh period. I said ok, but I was thinking oh no. What have I done wrong now? There wasn't anything I had done wrong, but Mr. Grady wanted to talk to me about my grades and my potential to do special things in life. At first I was a little puzzled and was wondering what he was talking about? Mr. Grady sat me down and gave me a one on one talk about my potential in life and he said that I was not giving my studies my all. I looked at him with a look of being disturbed and said what most kids say, "Come on Mr. Grady, I have seven periods, choir practice, band practice after school curricular activities and I did not have any more free time". He immediately said, "Do not give me any excuses; you can do what you want to do". As he continued to explain what he saw in me, I paid close attention to his prophetic views about me. I figured that this must be pretty important if Mr. Grady has called me in after school to discuss my grades and my life with me. To this day, I thank God for Mr. Grady. He challenged me to look deeper in myself and I began to expect more out of myself. My B grade went to an A and it remained there. My study habits carried on into three different college studies and four graduations, which ultimately transitioned me into ministry.

Achievements

What happens to those individuals who do not have a Mr. Grady to speak into their lives? Yes, I admire Michael Jordan, Michael Jackson, Mike Tyson, Tiger Woods, Oprah Winfrey and my very own Bishop T.D. Jakes for their accomplishments. The path that they have paved for us is great and I love them for what they have done. However, I do not confuse their achievements with who I am and where I am going. I am on the path to be the best Minister Johnnie Sanders that I am predestined to be. Those achievements may or may not happen for me, but I shall continue to be the best man of God that I can be. What bothers' me, are the improper role models that our youth have adopted as fine wine or gold or elegant lilies of today.

As I mentioned to you earlier, the lily is a very elegant and unique flower. This flower symbolized an ardor, which is something that brings feelings of great intensity and emotional warmth and passion. The Lily is a magnificent and beautiful flower that has such depth to it. In the 3rd book of Psalms 80:1 it reads, "For the director of music. To [the tune of] "The Lilies of the Covenant." Of Asaph: A psalm. Hear us, O Shepherd of Israel, you who lead Joseph like a flock; you, who sit enthroned between the cherubim, shine forth". Well the Lilies were a testimony, a psalm where the flock of people dwelt in between the cherubim (angel) of the mercy seat, where God met with His people. Imagine God sitting as King on His throne in His audience chamber. What a glorious resting place.

What happens when the sweet, good-natured, wonderful lilies run into that brick wall of obstacles, disappointments and shattered dreams? Do you give up? Do you become bitter with life? Do you begin to jump on the wrong side of the track? You know which track I'm talking about. The one where you get so fed up in life that you decide to choose to do wrong or venture off into that place where you know it is not you, but you're tired of doing the right thing. You're tired of being the good boy or good girl. You give into the lust of the eyes. You choose to accept the lust of the flesh. Truth in life, you hear that small whisper in your head that tells you, "go ahead and do it". Smoke that joint, get a drink, and get high at least once. Nobody is looking, who cares, life has thrown you lemons and you're tired of making lemonade. You want to drink the fine wines that you have seen others vast in. You ask the question, when is it going to be my turn to enjoy the finer vacations in life? Oh yes, the lust of eyes and the lust of the flesh do not escape the rich and the wealthy. You keep asking yourself, why do they keep looking over me for that movie role? How does he keeps getting a radio show and I gave him those jokes? If I only had a few more million dollars in my account, I could move in that area where I could really be in the mix. I have a good woman, but this is probably a once in a lifetime opportunity for me to get with her. Your good, educated, wealth, moral self is not thinking on the lines of the beautiful lily at that time, are you? Unfortunately, when you venture out and participate in that rosy, thorny bush, you get pricked and the deeds that you have done, it will come back upon you.

Rumors

There was this young man, whom we shall name Fred. Fred was a nice guy who was raised in a Christian family home and he was able to get a very nice education. He graduated cum lade from Xavier University and began working for a very prestigious law firm. He began to make a successful living and he married his high school sweetheart. They had two children a boy and a girl and he purchased this big, beautiful new home in the suburbs. Things were going pretty good for Fred and his family. Fred was very involved in the church choir and participated in many social events. Well, one day Fred was leaving church late one evening and some people saw him and began a rumor that Fred was having an affair with the choir director. This rumor was not true, but the implications started spreading like wild flowers in the fields. Eventually Fred and his wife were hit with this news and his wife reacted immediately as if she believed the rumors. After all, he would come home from rehearsal late and still singing songs. Fred could not believe the rumors nor could he believe his wife would think that the rumors were true. As you could imagine, this caused such a riff in their home and she took the kids and went to her mothers' house. Fred tried to convince his wife that these rumors were false and that she should believe him and not some people who are on the outside of their home. The word got around in the church and at the law firm that Fred and his wife were separated. Fred was in this place of disbelief and found it very difficult to continue to sing in the choir or even to attend church. I have always believed that a hot log in the fireplace will soon get cool, once it has been pulled out of the fire. Oh it will remain hot for a while, but its source of heat is no longer being provided. Fred began to listen to those whispering voices in his head that he was better than the critics and he started believing the lie that they said that he was. Fred was not a whore munger, or a cheat, or an adulterer. He was still Fred, but his perception of himself had changed. The weight of the lies in life began to wear him down. Fred began to say to himself, “maybe I ought to go out and some fun with a woman”, “maybe I ought do what they are accusing me of” he thought that if they are going to say these nasty things about him, then he should at least have some fun in the mean time. Truth in life, Fred goes out with a couple of ladies and tries to have a good time. Well, while Fred is out, some of his acquaintances sees him and reports back to their friends. You see, I told you it must have been true. Now I just want to point out to you that these so called acquaintances or friends, or associates, were in the same place, and at the same time that Fred was seen in. While out on the town, Fred came to himself and realized that he did not want to be in a place like this. He adopted the horrible label that people had spoken on him. He gathered his things and went home. Fred’s wife came to the house to get some things for the kids and noticed that Fred was very subdued and he was not saying much. He just stepped back and let her go where she wanted to go and get what she wanted to get from the house. As she moved back to the living room to say good-bye, she noticed that Fred was weeping. She tried to keep a stony heart, but something inside her was drawing her to him and she quietly asked Fred what was wrong. There was a wedding portrait of them on the wall and he was staring at the two of them, with her holding her beautiful bouquet of lilies. He said to her that you are so beautiful then and now. He said, "I remember when you were walking down the isle holding those beautiful lilies in your hand with a string of pearls draped around them and I could not believe that this beautiful angel is coming to me to be my bride for the rest of my life". His wife looked at the picture and looked at Fred and finally asked the question, "Were the rumors about you true"? Fred wiped his eyes, stood up tall, and walked towards his wife and boldly said no. Fred reached for her and touched her chin. She began weeping and hugged him with deep sorrow and gave him a passionate kiss. Fred apologized for the late hours and promised to call her if he would be leaving anywhere late in the future. The couple discussed the issues that were on the table and discussed preventive measures for future encounters when working with the opposite sex.

In this particular case, things worked out in the end for Fred and his wife, but how many times does people believe a lie and run with it. Friends, life is going to bring lies and un-truths up against you. You have to prepare yourself for the good and the not so good. It helps having a strong foundation with the Lord and having a circular of family and friends who really know you and have your back at all times. Even when the odds look against you, you need those remnant of people who knows the real you. Please remember to fear not, for God has given you a spirit of power, of love, and of a sound mind. God is on your side and HE will never leave you nor forsake you. Trust in HIM and lean not unto thy own understanding, but trust in the word that HE has given you in your bossom. For HE that has begun a good work in you shall perform it until the day of Jesus Christ. I pray to our Majestic God, whose voice holds together our universe. I pray for those who can barely walk under the stress and pressures of life. I pray for truth to come forth in all situations and I ask that you give the people the fortitude to continue along the pathway that you have predestined for us, before the creation of this world. I specifically want to pray for the lilies that have gone on for so long without being watered and nurtured. Please, dear LORD, give them strength and meet their most pressing needs. Through the intercession of Jesus, I ask these auspicious prayers, Amen!

Chapter 4

Loosed to Love, His Way

Matthew 16:19
And I will give unto thee the keys of the kingdom of heaven: and whatsoever thou shalt bind on earth shall be bound in heaven: and whatsoever thou shalt loose on earth shall be **loosed** in heaven.

Because of past unpleasant circumstances in life, we have placed walls and barriers around us and sometimes too much protection around our heart. There will be many times in life as a believer in Christ that one will feel like throwing in the proverbial towel. We all have felt a sense of failure, shame, defeat, rejection and a ton of emotions that have been conjured up within ourselves. Our emotions will affect our thoughts and actions toward others, whether we realize that or not. I want to talk about the specific keys in life and try to help you realize that you have a purpose in life. You can achieve heights beyond any measure that your mind has thought of. Learning how to love yourself will also matriculate into you loving others. I believe that with the Lord on your side, with confidence in yourself, and a genuine love in your heart, your actions will further propel you into your destiny.

There is this attractive couple that we will call Bill and Bridgett. Bill and Bridgett are middle class people, who have a son and a daughter. Bill and Bridgett are very active in their local church and community. The kids get good grades and are very well mannered. From the outside, they appear to be a solid, loving family, and they are. However, there is some dysfunction in every family. Whether we accept it or not, we all have something or someone we don't want to share or discuss with outsiders. Bill's issue was being hooked on pornography. He didn't mean to get so involved with it, but Bill felt that Bridgett was paying more attention to the kids than he was with him. As a kid, Bill was made to feel less than others as a kid. Bill did not get the love and attention as a child in his household and now that he is married with kids of his own, he is a little jealous of the attention and love that Bridgett gives their children. Well it might sound a little bizarre, but this is true. Bill's obsession with pornography began to affect his relationship with Bridgett and the kids. His past hurts tied him up into believing that Bridgett did not love him. He formed this image in his mind that she loved the kids more than him. Those childhood memories of bondage crippled his relationship with his new family. But for all the Bills out there, I have come to tell you that our King, and our Lord Jesus Christ, has loosed you. He has forgiven you of all your sins, all of your trespasses that you have committed.

Psalm 105:20 "The king sent and loosed him; [even] the ruler of the people, and let him go free".

Now the Kingdom of heaven is the spiritual of God and the ultimate place to receive love. Jesus himself is love. There is no one else like HIM. As HE came down from heaven and took on this ratcheted body of sin, His actions were love. As Jesus was beaten and whipped and spat upon and was nailed on that rugged cross, that was love. As Jesus hung there in the burning sun, loosing strength, dehydrating, and still being mocked on the cross, that was love. As He died and entered the pits of hell to set the captives free, as he snatched the keys of death from the enemy, as He removed the sting from the grave, which was love. I Corinthians 15:55 reads, O death, where is thy sing? O grave, where is thy victory? Please understand that Jesus died for you and I and He has empowered us to loose to love others.

Struggles

The myriad of trials, tribulations, and afflictions that a believer in Christ seems to encounter at every hand will sometimes lead many believers to feel that he or she is on the losing side of this game called life and that there is hardly anything left in us to put us over the top. Trials and tribulations have hit some of us so many times like a boxer, that we are literally punch-drunk. The scriptures declare in the book of II Timothy 3:12, Yea, and all that will live godly in Christ Jesus shall suffer persecution. We have all heard this scripture time and time again, yet while we are going through the valleys of life this scripture doesn't always ease the pain, nor do we feel like giving love. It would seem in our natural minds that there is some form of universal injustice here, when a believer who loves the Lord with all of his or her heart, soul, and mind has to go through the valleys of life. It is so much easier to love others when you're on the mountain top. The problems of the world seem smaller and we are able to handle an issue with ease. My brothers and sisters I have to confess that as a

Minister of the Gospel, we are not exempt from trouble, and sometimes because we are ministers, we suffer even more because of the call on our lives. However, when trouble hits us, it is difficult to share with others because after all we are the ones who are supposed to have it all together and we would not dare let others know that sometimes we are struggling to. It is our responsibility to carry the word of God. It is very frustrating to walk, talk, and breath the word of God and to still deal with struggles sometimes. I used to think that because someone was a minister or pastor that the Lord would make sure they would not be attacked as much because that person would be delivering His word. Sorry, that is not the case and I learned very quickly that I, as well as others, would be attacked even more because of our calling. As we work out the ailing pressures of life, we have to continue to share love in the mist of any pain that we may be experiencing. For me personally, I have to go over and beyond sometimes just to prove to others that I am nice and friendly. When you're under a public microscope, people are quick to label you or come to a conclusion about you that is false and they never took the time to talk to you or really hear your heart. Most of a Christian's struggles are private and not public and many Christians are struggling in places that others simply can't see. My brothers and sisters in Christ we will all go through struggles, but the devil's chief objective is to make you or I feel like we were born out of season, born under a bad sign, or that there is some dark ominous cloud following us throughout our lives. Please know that this is not true. The devil knows that the Lord has a plan and a purpose in your life and the devil is trying to prevent your prepared place. The devil is strategic and always on his mission to steal, to kill, and to destroy. He achieves his objective by keeping our struggles ever before us, he want us to believe that we are the only ones that are going through struggles. The enemy will steer you to look at how others seem to be sailing through life on flowery beds of ease, while you are moving at a snail's pace, and he wants you to see how others who are not living a Christian life are successful in their endeavors. It appears that they are prospering while you are still struggling. The enemy knows that we are living in the day of keeping up with the Jones, and he will use the fact that your car, which you drive to church every Sunday morning, is not as nice and not shining as the drug dealer's car on the corner. Maybe you are one of the faithful brothers and sisters in your spiritual walk and you are in church all of the time and you still don't have a spouse, and you look over at others who are out running the streets and it appears to you that this sister have met Prince Charming or the brother is able to meet his queen with ease. Please do not look on the outside of someone else's situation because you can very well be fooled. Not saying that nobody is having true success or true love and happiness, but what I am saying is don't be so quick to desire something or someone and God hasn't place you in position to receive what or who He has in store for you.

Success

No body is exempt! The drug dealers are struggling as well, but they are struggling with out Jesus! We may struggle for a little while, but we are struggling in victory. To struggle in the walk with Jesus, is a different way of struggling. It is a strengthening to our well being. We as Christian believers have been anointed to prosper; we have been anointed to succeed. The Lord knows your heart and desires and He shall provide it to you, according to His riches and glory for your life.

The ability to love is a choice that we make. It's also an action word. I can say I love you every day all day, but it doesn't grow and build until I actually show you. It sounds good and feels good to be told the words that someone loves you, but it has a more profound impact in your life when it is displayed. Love should be shown to everyone, but especially to your kindred, your family, your relatives and your church family. John 13:35 says, by this shall all [men] know that you are my disciples, if you have love one to another. The world looks at how we, as Christians, treat others and our display of love will draw them to be apart and learn and to accept Jesus as their person Lord and savior. In 1 Peter 4:8 ... Love covers a multitude of sins. It is important to reach out to family members and love them with the love of the lord. Just like individuals of the world, family members watch you and your actions and you are their only living bible that they see. We should show and share love with even the family members that get on your last nerve. I remember for Christmas, one of my uncles came over to our home and he was drunk. I was playing with my brand new train set in the living room. I spent about two hours connecting all the tracks and putting in the train depot and the bells at the railroad crossings. My uncle walked in and stepped on my train tracks and broke them into two pieces. My mouth flew open and I yelled out, "Get off my tracks!" Well my mother heard me and she came to see what was going on. She pulled my uncle into the kitchen and sat him down and made some coffee. Needless to say, I was upset, hurt, angry and all the above of emotions. The next meeting between my uncle and I was an opportunity for me to show him love. Even at a tender young age, I realized that he did not mean to hurt me, and it did hurt. I made a choice, even as a young boy to love him in spite of the anger I felt before. Because of the actions of love and forgiveness that I displayed to my uncle, on our future encounters, he remembered how I treated him each time and when I became a young man, he asked me to take him to church one Sunday. I loved my uncle and I knew he loved me, but like so many people, he did not know how to show the love of God, in the true biblical since of agape love. My actions toward him allowed him to remove any defenses that he may have conjured up in his mind and allowed love to saturate his heart. My love showed him that I was more concerned about how I could meet his needs and feelings and that I did not have anything stewing in my soul.

People respond better when they are happy and I believe happiness keeps you smiling and your responses are sweet. The trials of life keep us focused and strong. The sorrows and disappointments that happens to us, keeps us human. As we strive to do well, but at times we fall short, those failures will keep us humbled. However, when we achieve success and accomplish our goals, we get a pep in our step and our face begin to start glowing, but only "the power of GOD" keeps us going!

Father I pray that every band be loosed, every mouth be opened and every heart filled with your love. I pray that the word of God causes an earth quake to loose all the blessings that have been held up by our enemy. May your Believers receive the harvest that has been held up for so long by the enemy. Loose that man, Loose that woman and let them go, in Jesus name. Devil you have no place here, for the Lord God is the King of Kings and the Lord of Lords and the enemies of this world shall become scattered as the Lord loose His love upon us all. For we love you Lord and we thank you. Amen!

Chapter 5

Lord and Savior

2 Peter 3:18

But grow in the grace and knowledge of our Lord and Savior Jesus Christ. To him be glory both now and forever! Amen.

Do you know Him? Ok, so you do know Him. Let me ask you another question, how close do you walk with Him? How deep is your relationship? I ask these questions because sometimes we need to be reminded where we are and reevaluate our relationship with Him. Let's call it a self-check. If we are seeking the Lord daily and praying without ceasing, you can find comfort that you are on the right track. We all need to know where we are in the grand scheme of things if our life. We need to hear what He is telling us follow His direction.

Following the Lord's direction becomes a little distorted when we stop praying like we should. His voice gets dimmer when we slack off in our reading the bible. Sometimes we begin new journeys without even consulting the Lord and when trouble breaks out, fear comes over us. We begin to second-guess, and third guess ourselves. "Who is among you that fears the LORD, that obeys the voice of His servant, that walks in darkness and has no light? Let him trust in the name of the LORD and rely upon his God" Isaiah 50:10. The Spirit of God should lead our life. When we walk with Him, we can sense His presence. When others see us they can see we are living victoriously, and our outward characteristics reflect the life of a person who is free. Free from hurt, pain, and disappointment, free from the lies that has been told on you. It is such a joy and blessing to be able to walk in this state of mind. However, what if you couldn't sense His presence? What if God, for some reason, suspended His blessings? What would you do if you were faithfully following God and suddenly all external circumstances turned sour? I mean the world that you know turns upside down and inside out. What are you going to do? Who are you going to turn to? I have a suggestion, please turn to Jesus Christ, my personal Lord and Savior.

Let me share some real stories with you that will help you to lean onto the Lord with confidence and humbleness. There was this family that went through some extremely dark periods in their family life. There were days of continual trials and tribulation that this family were forced and wisely began quoting the scripture Isaiah 50:10. The father become drastically ill and was off from work for months and their finances were dreadfully dwindled. The wife lost her grandmother and the kids were having issues with their grades and needed some personal attention. This family felt perplexed and bewildered and didn't understand what was happening to them. They didn't know if it would be easier to deal with the sharp pain of being delivered from a situation that God was taking them through or to accept the nagging pain of staying in their dilemma. Isaiah is asking if there is a believer, is there somebody who fears the Lord as they walk in darkness. Isaiah is not referring to the darkness of sin that we can easily put our finger on or even the darkness of this world. No, no, Isaiah is talking about the darkness of uncertainty and insecurity that weighs on our hearts and minds when we do not understand what is going on in our life. It appears to our humanly flesh and our sin conscience eyes that our Lord and Savior has suspended His conscious blessings and the hedge of protection has been lifted.

What would you do in this situation? How would you handle the next adversary? No matter how dark your situation gets, the Lord always will provide you some light. He will lead you out of darkness, but we must be willing to take that one step that He is showing us. As we keep taking more and more steps, the pathway becomes clearer and brighter. If you see a snake in the road, you will most likely move over to the sidewalk or turn around and go the other way. However, the Lord does not want you to turn around in the darkness. The Lord knows you may become fearful, but fear not and press toward the direction where He is leading you. Trust where He is leading you and keep walking. Trust and walk in the past manifestation that the Lord has brought you out of the storm of darkness. Remember that if the Lord brought you out of darkness a year ago, or seven years ago, He is faithful and just to bring you out again. As a believer, I do my very best to never make major decisions about temporary circumstances. As I wait and pray and watch, and pray some more, I keep looking for my break through. My faith and belief is that God has not left me. He has only suspended His conscious presence so that my faith will not rest on feelings or be established by unique experiences or blessings. The stretching and the trying of my faith have been matured by the level of circumstances that I have overcome.

The family continued to hold on and trust in the Lord and the husband's health improved. The wife prayed and received comfort from family members and church members and she dealt with the death of her grandmother. The children were able to get in an after school-tutoring program and their grades improved. In their darkness of life, the family did not stay in that doubtful place, but they continued to pray and looked for the light to guide them into that blessed place.

Adversary

Our heavenly father is either Lord of all in our lives or he is not Lord at all! We as believers in the "good book" need to understand and expect the enemy to come at us. It does not mean that we wait for horrible times. We have been taught that we ought not to be ignorant of the devils devices. Wherever the Lord spreads His abundant life, there will always be a crowd! People recognize when they see something good happening and they will flock to it. Whether they are believers of the gospel or not, people enjoy being around winners and the popular.

I must confess as an ardent believer in Christ and one who has been called to break the bread of life to others that sometimes I even feel that trouble seems to have my name, social security number, address, cell phone and my email. The enemy is waging an all out attack on believers and churches in this day of enlightenment and this day of information. The ability to send information all over the world within a matter of seconds has caused an epidemic of free spirit ness and elusiveness to bombard homes and business with unwanted information. People can gain information from the good the bad and the not so good with a push of a few button. With ease you can access pornography, music, movies, how to make a bomb, self-training in firearms, and self-healing to horoscopes and spirit worlds. Some of the snapshots that we see on the internet, we form an opinion of ourselves and we assess our own life, and we check out how we're measuring up against those of our peers, or those in China, Australia, Africa, New Jersey, New York, Florida, California or Dallas. Not all of the information is bad, but it does seem that the more information that we obtain about what is going on, we seem to validate ourselves by other people. As a minister, I have had the privilege of visiting many, many churches and I have seen a profound affect that the church has allowed certain aspects of the world to come in. Some of the doctrines have been watered down to fit certain congregations. God's word has not changed! God's standard has not changed.

Peoples' beliefs, social status, circumstances and opinions change and they want you to conform to their way. However, we are the steadfast people who conform to the word of God. The churches of old would celebrate when one soul came to the altar to be saved and they would rejoice and shout with a voice of triumph for that one. There would be praising, singing and thankfulness that would spread from the pulpit to the back wall where the fire extinguisher would be hanging. When I see the lack of respect from members and visitors during an altar call, it does anger me to see people get up and walk out of service. The man or woman of God would be speaking and people would get up as if they were not doing anything wrong. It breaks my heart to see a pastor of a congregation of eleven members being looked upon as less important to the kingdom of God; and not as important as that pastor of a congregation of eleven thousand members. So many churches have gotten so caught up in numbers that we fail to respect what the other pastor is doing. In 1 Samuel 29:5 Is not this David, of whom they sang one to another in dances, saying, Saul slew his thousands, and David his ten thousands. Saul should have been thankful to be used to kill a thousand men who were attacking him. This is not a competition. David did not brag or gloat about what he had achieved. In the mist of the battle, I doubt it very seriously that David was standing there counting how many men he had just slain. He was in a fight and he was fulfilling his duty to his leader. When the day was over, both soldiers were standing victoriously as winners. David has personal assignment to fight in this war and he fulfilled it. Those of us in ministry sometimes will miss our personal assignment from God because we are so busy keeping up with how God is using someone else. Cheer that brother or sister on as you continue to finish your assignment. The Lord chooses whom He wants, when He wants, and how He wants to use them in His own timing. We should continue to pray for them and thank God for them because they have been equipped by God to do that job for such a time as this. We cannot do it all and we should not want to. Many believers spend a lot of time in seeking validation, affirmation, certification, and substantiation from others than we do seeking the face of God. Matthew 25:21 “His lord said unto him, Well done, thou good and faithful servant; thou hast been faithful over a few things, I will make thee ruler over many things.”

It is God alone who validates us, God alone who certifies

us, God alone who affirms us, and God alone who substantiates us. God is no respect of person. He loves us all and He gives gifts of different stature and different places in our lives. You may not be called to build the building. You may be called to administer the work within the building. You may be called to provide the food within the building. We serve a God that sees all, knows all, and can do all. We do not serve a God that we can rush, nor can we manipulate Him into doing what we think is right. Our Lord and Savior do not tell his children to compromise to make it over or to fit in. We are equipped to stand with the armor of God. We should know that He is our present help.

Resilient

When you know you've heard from God, be resilient. Stand on His word that He has given you. Remember that things worth having are never easily attained. When you are in the midst of a struggle and you are not sure which way you should turn or you find yourself weakening, remind yourself that God has given you the grace to succeed at whatever He's called you to do! This means being sensitive to His voice. God's voice is not like a hammer pounding on your head; it's more like a gentle prompting within. Paul says, "But now we are delivered from the law, that being dead wherein we were held; that we should serve in newness of spirit [promptings] and not in the oldness of the letter". (Romans 7:6) Now you can ignore His promptings, disobey them, argue with them or even try to postpone them, but when you do that "you" end up putting more on yourself than you can bear. Your prayer should be that God changes your conditions or that God conditions you for change!

There will be some interesting surprises to many saints when they make it to heaven. As I observe how we treat one another and as I listen to the conversations of others with the intent of understanding the way people think. Understanding how to love someone is a precious gift. Understanding your purpose in life is exuberating and when we get to heaven, you will discover that many of the people that you thought would not be in heaven made it there. Understanding that there are certain things that need to happen and it is apart of that person's purpose. Some of you will be shocked to also find out that many of those that you knew would be in heaven are not there. You want to accept Jesus, as Lord and Savior and you need to walk with Him. Practice His daily principals and receive His word. Now when you learn what your purpose is, you grab hold to that purpose and move toward your promise. The Lord is faithful to water and nurture the seed that is planted and you have to keep working and moving and you will see your harvest. Do not fear where you have not been. If you think back on your life, the Lord has trained you on the backside of the desert and has prepared you to go into the unknown and unfamiliar to your eyes. Walk in it by your spirit and trust Him.

Memories

You may have failed many times when you have tried to step out on faith on a thought or an idea that you know would be useful. Every time you try to go on and leave the idea alone, it keeps coming back in your mind. Take a walk with me down memory lane. Remember how many times you fell down the first time you tried to walk. Well, maybe you don't remember how many times you fell or how many times you have seen a baby that is close to you fall? You know that it was a number of times that the baby failed, but eventually they began to hold on to something or someone and began to walk. Do you remember the first time that you began to learn how to swim? You were slapping water everywhere and you thought you were going to drown. Did you hit the baseball the first time you swung your bat? How many times did you kick the ball before it went where you wanted it to go? Many baseball players, who are considered heavy hitters, are players who hit the most home runs. However, if you check out their misses, you will find that they also struck out a lot. R. H. Macy failed seven times before his store in New York caught on. English novelist John Cracey got 753 rejection slips before he published 564 books. Babe Ruth struck out 1,330 times, but he also hit 714 home runs. Nike has new commercials airing about the amount of attempts athletes take shots at the basket. The commercial shows how many reps were taken in exercising, how many trips in the playoffs before finally arriving or playing in the championship game. When stepping out on faith, do not focus on if you may fail. Focus on the opportunity that is present before you and try to achieve your goals and the purpose that has been placed in you. It would be a shame if you concern yourself with failure and miss the chances to succeed by not even trying.

In a performance-oriented culture such as ours, failure belts us like a punch in the stomach. Repeated failure often results in a knockout blow, and many people give up altogether. Let's face it, we all have egos, but how strong do we allow the ego to take over us? As Comedian W. C. Fields once quoted at a comedy club, "If at first you don't succeed, then quit. There's no use in being a fool about it." The problem is that a life with little failure is a life of little risk. You have to be willing to take some risk in order to achieve what has not been done. We can live our life in a fish bowl or in such security walls that we miss out on what the Lord has purposed for us. This type of life may appear to offer safety and security, but it actually leads to guilt, boredom, further apathy and even low feelings of self-esteem. "God did not give us the spirit of fear, but a spirit of power, and of love, and of a sound mind." (2 Timothy 1:7). God designed and commissioned us to be productive; many times that demands faith and risk. Trust in the Lord, even if you fail at something. Sometimes it takes several attempts before you finally get it. If you want unlimited victory then give God unlimited praise!

Taking a chance or risks in life always puts your mind in a race of thought patterns of concern. You go through the motions of pros and cons and you try to make calculated risks.

Once you have put together your plan, you must take the stance of progression and walk out your plan. Habakkuk 2:2 says, "And the LORD answered me, and said, write the vision, and make [it] plain upon tables, that he may run that readeth it." You have to also prepare for opposition and take a strong stand and a strong stance for God. I say this because doing anything that the Lord has called you to do will always attract persecution. 2 Timothy 3:12 reads, "Yes, and all that will live godly in Christ Jesus shall suffer persecution." Get in your mind that the enemy has prepared to fight against you. Because you have been chosen and you have accepted your Lord and Savior and is choosing this lifestyle, which is to follow Christ, your walk will offend those who does not follow Christ or don't believe in the power of His resurrection. Some of us are tired of the games that people play, and we are tired of the reality shows and the shows of religion where everybody talks a good game, but their lifestyle has no fruit or power in anything that they do.

My brother and sister in Christ there are no instant breakthroughs; the only way to breakthrough is to go through. Go through without fear and trembling. The Lord has shown us in biblical stories and scriptures of how He greatly used men and women of God and how they were greatly opposed. The book says, "That in the end, we win." Revelation 15:2 And

I saw as it were a sea of glass mingled with fire: and them that had gotten the victory over the beast .... So knowing that we have the victory, push away those fears, stand up and take what the Lord has in store for you. Saints you were chosen to achieve more and you are blessed to strive to the other side of that storm. Don't you dare weary in well doing and you will receive the prize that has been waiting for you. Trust in our Lord and Savior and remember, the things you pay more attention to will get bigger in your life. If you pay attention to the problems of life, the bigger life's problems will become. But when you focus on the promises of God, His word begins to matriculate in your life and the problems get smaller and His voice gets bigger.

Father we just want to say, Thank you for being our Lord and Savior. Amen!

Chapter 6

Lowly Place

Proverbs 3:34
Surely he scorneth the scorners: but he giveth grace unto the lowly.

There are different life experiences that will bring you to a lowly place. Life's issues and training is unavoidable, and this is in the "valley lows" for the Christian terminology. In my life I have gone through many valley lows, but I have lived in the blessings of the mountain top experiences more. Hallelujah! As a teenager, I was a member of the Fellowship of Christian Athletes and the Lord laid it on my heart to have a bible study in my home for other teenagers. The bible study began with two of my friends and me. We would just gather in my parents' living room and began with a word of prayer. Then we would sing a couple of songs and then we would begin reading passages of scriptures and have discussions afterward. We would end the study time with prayer and my mother would have sandwiches, punch and cookies for us in the kitchen. The bible study grew to about 50 teenagers that would come over. Yes, it became very crowded really fast and we began searching for a larger place to me. We would meet in the school gym or library conference room to continue the study. The Lord blessed us tremendously and we were very pleased with the success that had taken place with what started out so small. Well, before I could graduate high-school, a very bad sickness took over my body. I received a tentative scholarship to La. Tech University and my major was going to be engineering, but I was unable to obtain my scholarship. The sickness came from out of nowhere and I had fever everyday of 102 to 103 degrees consistently. My parents brought me to several hospitals and the doctors ran several tests on me, but they could not explain my condition. So, they would discharge me and we would try another hospital. We finally went to a major hospital in New Orleans and the doctors didn't run any test on me at the time. They just looked at me, checked my pulse and temperature and whisked me away to the emergency room. When I finally awoke from the medicine, I had tubes in my nose, tubes in my arms and I was admitted into intensive care.

This is where the journey began, because my duration in the hospital would last for three detrimental months. The pain that invaded my body was something that I had never experienced before. The doctors did not know what was really wrong with me, but they knew that something was going on wrong with this young man. Everyday, tests were run and blood was being drawn until my veins finally collapsed. My appetite was gone and my physical condition went from 170 pounds of solid muscle to 124 pounds with in two weeks. The doctors were trying everything that they could think of and they even flew in specialist to try and treat me, as well as study my condition. After a period of time, an infection formed in my lungs and the infection sealed itself within a section of my lungs and the antibiotics could not reach it. So the doctors performed what they called a "tapping" of my chest. They doctor and the nurse came to my bed and pulled out this needle and syringe that was about a foot and a half long all together. The doctor should have never let me see that needle because I was about to pass out. To see something that big that has to enter your body, come on, you're going to have some self-preservations of continuing. The nurse would keep me focused on her by talking to me. I could feel the needle a little bit, but I was trying to be strong. The doctor pulled out of my back a tube of yellow infection. That was the first syringe. It was so much stuff inside of me that she had to use a second syringe to get the rest out of me.

This procedure was successful and I began to feel better almost overnight. My color began to come back into my face, my appetite began to increase and I started gaining a little weight. The fevers began to slow down, but there was something still wrong inside my body and the doctors would not tell me. The doctors shared information with my parents and my parents would try to explain without scaring me. I knew something was going on, but I could not get anyone to tell me. Because I started feeling better, I wanted to go home so I could start training again, so I would not loose my scholarship at La. Tech University. The doctors said that I would not run again, at least not at the level to play football. The doctors didn't really think that I would live past the age of 25. As you may have gathered at this point, this was an extremely "Valley Low" for me. Things were not looking good for me. One month has gone by and the doctors wanted to put a "Chest Tube" in me to clear out any remaining infections. Oh my God, this was from the devil. That is all I could think of. I didn't even know what a "Chest Tube" was, but let me tell you, I most certainly do now.

My mother did not want this procedure done to me and she tried to convince the doctors that there is another way. Well the doctors were afraid of loosing me and they knew my mother was reacting upon her emotions. My mother was a nurse and technician at this hospital and the doctors knew she would interfere. So the doctors planned to keep my mother busy with tests and graphs and other possible plans because my mother and father would visit me faithfully and often everyday. While my mother was busy, the doctors rolled me into an adjourning room. Please notice that I did not say operating room. This room was cold and I noticed the glaring stares on the nurse's faces. They looked very concerned for me. As a patient, I had been there for quite some time and I had become a special case, so all the nurses knew me and treated me. Well the doctor told me that they were going to do this procedure and it would only take a few minutes. I asked the doctors, "Where was my mother"? They said that she would be in the room in a few minutes, just lie down and relax, so I said ok. I rolled onto my stomach and the doctors began to deaden my back. After a few short minutes, I felt the scalpel open my back. I said to the doctors, "that's cold, I could feel air". The doctor tried to stick this tube into my lung, but it could not enter because of the shrinking of my muscles from the 170 pounds to the 124 pounds. He could not get the tube passed my ribs, so he tried to pry my ribs apart. Oh my God, did I scream. I yelled out, "what are you doing, this really hurts". As I looked to my left, I could see the faces of the nurses and they were crying. At this point, I had a strong sense that something was going wrong and I wanted them to stop. Well, I could not breathe anymore and I said to the doctors with my last breath, "Doc, I can't breathe. I'm going to die". The doctors were trying desperately to save me and I could feel the doctors' knuckles and his wedding ring pressing against my insides. As I lay on the table, I could not talk, I could not move, and all I could do was look at the weeping nurses and I could hear the doctors panicking. There was a beeping monitor hooked to me and I could hear a continuous flat-line sound. As I closed my eyes, a peace came upon me. I felt the presence of the Lord with me and I began to talk with Him spiritually. The conversation that I had with the Lord was, "Lord, if you say that it is time to come on home, please bid me to come". The next thing that I could feel was the doctor ramming this tube in me and tearing my stomach lining. Oxygen finally came back into my body and I regained consciousness. The bed that I was on was soaked with blood and I could hear the nurses cheerfully saying,

"Johnnie is not dead, he is alive"! When I finally awoke, my mother was walking up to my bed with tears in her eyes. My body was hooked to a machine and I was extremely groggy. By the abundance of my mothers' tears, I knew I was in very bad shape. When my father arrived at my bedside, his tears began to fall like a waterfall and he could not control them. Looking at them, I could only imagine what I looked like. Something from a horror movie I supposed. It was obvious that I was an atrocious site, but I was alive. The devil should have killed me when he had the chance.

Recovery

Well my recovery time was another two months and I had to fight demonic spirits, fear, doubt, never giving up, never bowing down to the voices. Oh yes, voices that were telling me to kill myself. Voices that were telling me that "I was never going to have a normal life; even more voices saying I would never be blessed following Jesus". When I began to get my strength, I would take that machine and roll it down the hallway with me as I walked. I had a routine everyday that I would presume. In my recovery time, I ministered and witnessed to doctors, nurses, janitors, visitors, patients, delivery people and anyone who would stop and listen to me. I had to fight and that was my way of fighting. I had to preach to myself, if no one else was going to be around. Several nurses and doctors were saved as I would lead them through the sinners' prayer as they accepted the Lord as their Savior. In my daily routine, I noticed this peculiar young man that would sit in the same location everyday. He was paralyzed from the waist down, but that was not what made me notice him.

He had a look upon his face as if he had given up on life and he was in the corner, smoking weed. I could not believe my eyes or my nose. I introduced myself to him and he told me his name. I boldly asked him to tell me why he was sitting in this hospital smoking weed and what happened to him. He explained that he was from Mississippi and he was working part time at this local grocery store and these guys would come by and harass the owner from time to time. The way that he described the store, it was more or less like a community store that was very small, but was much needed in the community. He asked this group of young guys to leave the man alone and to go away. My new friend was a big guy before he was paralyzed and figured he would help out. These guys were apparently in a local gang, so they challenged him to a fight. He did not want to fight them; he just wanted them to leave. He said they left and later the bread delivery truck came to deliver the bread shipment. As he began helping with the bread delivery, one of the guys came back to the store and stabbed this young man in his back. He said he didn't realize that he was stabbed at the time, but he knew he was hit. So he grabbed the guy in the gang and beat him down. When he finished, the guy in the gang jumped up and ran away. He started to walk back into the store and he started getting light headed and he dropped to his knees. The storeowner came to him and told him to lie down because he had a knife in his back. The ambulance came and rushed him to the hospital and he woke up paralyzed. He was now in a lowly place.

Man that is awful, this is what I said to him. So then I said to him, "Now explain to me why are you smoking weed". He said that the medication that he is taking is not strong enough to stop the pain and it didn't agree with his body and the weed stopped the pain. He even said that the doctors supplied him the weed. I didn't believe it, but I continued to talk to him everyday. My parents would bring him fruit, just like they brought me fruit. The witnessing about Jesus everyday and the open love from my parents convinced this young man to except Jesus Christ as his personal Lord and Savior. The next thing you know, he began to get feelings in his leg. This was great news because the doctors were considering amputating his legs off. The power of the Holy Spirit had moved and the miracle of the Lord had taken place.

After three long months, my discharge papers were finally handed to my father and he helped me into his truck and we went home. My rehabilitation process was just beginning. It took me about a year and a half to finally be able to walk, and then run again. There was a lot of hard work and dedication that I had to put forth into a healthy body again. You may be asking what was the cause, what was going on with you. Honestly, the doctors do not know. The only thing that did surface was the fact that I caught pneumonia in this process and that was cured. Well I lost my scholarship to La. Tech University, but I didn't stop dreaming, I didn't stop having goals and I have so many goals to achieve today. I learned at a young age that most of our struggles are private and not public. The whole time that I was sick, my family and friends were not allowed to come and see me. Towards the end of the recovery period, a couple of my prayer brothers came with my parents. But my siblings were not allowed to see me in that condition. The blessed assurance in all of this is that I was able to get my associates degree in Computer Science and Accounting. I was able to also graduate from an Engineering school and attain my 2nd Class Engineering license. I was able to play football, track, semi-pro baseball and I have received my Bachelors of Arts and Science degree from Dallas Baptist University. Glory to God!

Returning

So I have shared just some of the blessings in my life and trust me, there are many more. What have you gone through? Have it made you feel as if you cannot go on? Don't give it up. Jesus is a habit breaker and a difference maker. Whatever has been a pattern in your life, it stops today. Whatever was a generational curse in your family's life, it will no longer continue. Some of us forget who we are and where we came from. You didn't always do the things that you are doing. You didn't always act like a fool when you went out with your friends. Life has hit you so many times that you have given up or decided to do your own thing. Stand up and fight back! Come back to yourself, that person who really makes a difference in your world is still waiting on your return. In the book of Luke 15:17-18 "When he came to his senses, he said, How many of my father's hired men have food to spare, and here I am starving to death! I will set out and go back to my father and say to him: Father, I have sinned against heaven and against you." The Prodigal Son came to himself and remembered who he was and he remembered what he left. He knew what was back at home and it was a life of abundance, so he headed back in the direction of home. The son didn't get into trouble because he was a bad kid. He got into trouble because he left the guidance and the safety of his father.

Leaving the security of guidance, direction and safety will always allow the enemy to come in and trick you. Satan waits for you to leave that hedge of protection and venture out on you own. He entices you to be drawn away by your own lusts. Unfortunately, when you heed to his call, you always end up losing the very blessing that sustained you for all this time and you deviate from what God has called you to be. The Prodigal Son connected himself to a citizen(s) of that foreign country. He chose the wrong person(s) to hang with. He listened to the wrong voice. Do you want to know where you are spiritually? Check out who your friends are, look at whom you are taking advice from. Proverbs 1:10 says, "My son, if sinners entice you, do not give in to them". The Prodigal Son began to want what his friends began to share with him. He wanted what he saw they had. The son stopped looking for his father for help and guidance. While he was in his father's house he never missed a meal. In this new place that he found himself in, the bible said that he longed for the pods of the pigs. He was in unfamiliar territory and he was trying to meet a legitimate need in an illegitimate place. Thank God, this young man finally came to himself and he remembered who he was. It was not too late for him and it is not too late for you. If you hear that small, quaint voice speaking to you, don't harden your heart. Don't get puffed up and proud. Humble yourself and go back to which cometh your help. The moments you stop being selfish and stop saying give me this or give me that, the sooner you can receive from the Lord when you start saying Father forgive me.

There are so many people who hit the lowly place and they do not know what to do next or how to handle the lowly situation. This is a word to men and women who wants to find the secret of life, who wants to be a success. I have never yet met young people who didn't want to be successful. In my experience with young people no one has ever said,

"My ambition is to be a bum down on skid row." The way to success is to trust in the Lord with all your heart, and act upon the thoughts and gifts that He has given you. God has given you a reasonable mind and expects you to use it, but don't rely on your thoughts alone. You will need divine guidance and wise counsel before making large decisions. If there has been something or someone ailing you and you feel like life is unbearable, hold on before hastily making that decision. In the words of my Pastor, Bishop T. D. Jakes, "Someone else can play the very bad hand that life has dealt you and win!"

Model Family

Let me explain another family's dilemma. There was a young middle class couple, who appeared to be the perfect model family. You know the idea model that has been depicted by American standards, a husband and wife with 2.5 kids and a two story house with the white picked fence and two car garages. The family is living in the right neighborhood, where the kids can get the best education and there are community parks available. Parks where there are actually swings, and merry-go-rounds, with sea-saws for the kids to play on and an Olympic size pool. A public basketball court that is paved and the goals have real nets on them. This young man was a stockbroker and he was very successful. His family lived a peaceful life that was filled with prosperity, blessings and dignity and was very well respected. Without warning, this family's household was changed and turned upside down. The stock market crashed and all of their investments and 401k's were lost and his immediate finances were put on hold until the bank could grasp a hold to the disaster. His wife was picking up the kids from school in the SUV when she received the phone call from her husband. She became seriously stressed and she could not focus on the road because of the plethora of tears that streamed down her face. It began to rain and she did not adjust her driven and she swerved to keep from hitting an on coming car, but ran into a pole. The kids were not buckled up in their seat belts and were thrown forward out of the windshield. She was hospitalized, but the kids didn't make it. The husband rushed to the hospital only to find out the terrible news that had taken place. He tried to deal with everything that had happen to his family and he felt himself spiraling down fast and he cried out to the Lord for help, but he didn't receive an answer. The family lost their house, and the hospital bills forced them to sell their cars. His family and friends came to comfort him, but their recovery took too long for most of them, so they soon stopped coming by and stopped calling. This family life was never the same and they had to deal with where they were now. They were in a very lowly place and they needed to trust the Lord that He was with them. Things improved after a period of time, but no where near the level of success they once lived. So what do you do when you have hit a lowly place and when you come out, you have not been placed in a better situation than before all of these tumultuous things happened? You must first look toward Him for peace and direction. Let your requests be made known unto Him. Write down where you are and then write down where you want to go. Write down what you can not achieve on your own, but believe that He can make you requests happen. You can start journalizing your process and progress with timelines. As you come to a milestone, check it off. Keep a continued assessment of your life and re-evaluate yourself as often as you need to. You may not understand where you are or why you had to endure such pain, but the lowly place experience is all for your good. For the Lord said in Romans 8:28, "that all things work together for good to them that love God, to them who are the called according to [His] purpose." The couple may not have understood there lowly place, but there life was changed for a divine purpose and it is best for them to continue to trust in the Lord and if He never brings everything back to them, He is still good.

Father in the name of Jesus, I encourage my brothers and sisters to stand boldly upon the word of God. Lord you know what they are in need of and you know what needs to be removed. Lord you reign over the heathen and you sit upon the throne of righteousness. We will sing praises unto you because you are the Lord of hosts. You are the God of Abraham, Isaac and Jacob. May your will be done in our lives today and forever more. Amen!

Chapter 7

Ladies and Gentlemen

Ester 2:17 / Judges 5:29 / Isaiah 47:7

In today's world of dating and quest for relationships, I find it very interesting in the approach that men have towards women and the approach that women have towards men. My, my, my times have changed from the days of courtships and men wooing women. The dating games have changed, the expectations have changed and rules have changed. So many people today pursue after someone for the wrong reasons, in my humble opinion. People are not looking into a relationship of someone who has substance. More dating relationships are based on how the person looks, what do they drive, how long is her hair, what is their skin tone, how much money do they have, or they decide that none of that matters to me. We are just going to kick it for a little while and just have some casual sex. Where are the standards that women and men used to have towards one another? Where are the lace and pearls that ladies used to wear? Where are the sweet fragrances on the beautiful ladies that women once wore? Where are the men in fine suits? Where are the men that wear slacks and polished shoes and button down shirts? These people are still out there, but the world has portrayed such a strong, negative image of the people who are not looking lady like are like a gentleman. Men are not holding the door open for women like they used to. Men are not taking their lady to dinner and paying for the meal like they used to. So many women today do not know how to cook. Ladies, if you want to be treated like a lady, you have to act like one. You have to accept nothing less than to be treated like a queen. Not snuddy or stuck up, but having the standard and respect in your life that you walk with grace and elegance. When a man looks at you, he should want to know more about you. He should pursue this wonderful lady of distinction. To my brothers who want the respect of a woman and the honor of walking like a man. Men have to stand for something positive. You have to have visions, goals, dreams and aspirations. Women do not want a man who is not going anywhere or who is not doing anything. Men, when God said that He has designed this beautiful woman from your side to be here for you and to be your help meet, that means that you have to be doing something in order for her to help you meet that goal. Whatever your goal is, the woman is designed to help you achieve your goal(s). My sisters are achieving more goals today than ever before without a man. I believe this is happening because men are not doing what they have been called to do. Sorry my brothers, it might be tight, but it is right. You can look at statistics; you can watch talk shows or listen to radio shows and the evidence will be in your face. I hear some of you saying that those statistics are wrong, take a nice walk downtown. Just start looking around for yourself and you will see the large number of ladies who are in charge and not waiting on us men to stand up and step up to the plate. We as men have not been responsible enough with our roles in society. As a whole, the dilapidation of men standing and steering our homes, education, spiritual walk and finances into the proper direction has caused us to be looked upon as incapable or inadequate. Because of this slide in the quality of men, we have many articles with titles like, "Where have the good men gone?" "A good man is hard to find." Men, we have to start taking one step at a time to do better and to help the next man as you take steps in the right direction. With that said, ladies you are a queen and we take notice on how you take care of yourself and also we noticed that you have prepared yourself for prosperity.

A Queen

Queen Esther was a beautiful woman that not only beat out other women to become queen to the king, but she carried herself like a lady. With the help of her uncle, Mordecai, she was in the prepared place at the appropriate time. Esther was a woman of wisdom and she was able to receive counseling of Hegai, who was a custodian of the women being observed. She was a lady of lace, who was in the proper place to allow the king to choose her. Esther, along with other women, was prepared for twelve months with perfumes and preparations to meet the king. Ladies, it's true that being attractive does meet a need of men. However, that is not the only aspects of a lady that men take into consideration. Men really like the fact that a woman is smart. She and he can have a positive, intellectual conversation at times, as well as having fun at other times. Queen Esther was smart and she handled a difficult situation that was before her. Queen Esther learned of the plot to kill her uncle Mordecai, which was more of an attack on the Jews. Queen Esther could not just save herself in the long run of this hate and scandal. She had to respond with a thought out plan. For failure to act responsively would jeopardize the purpose for which she had become queen. So Queen Esther used wisdom and the favor on her life to setup a feast to bring the perpetrator before her king. Esther 5:8 reads, "If I have found favor in the sight of the king, and if it pleases the king to grant my petition and fulfill my request, then let the king and Haman come to the banquet, which I will prepare for them and tomorrow I will do as the king has said". Queen Esther first, humbly asked for permission and then she was prepared to cook. Now she walked out her plan and she did not step over her boundary of trying to rule over her king. She knew that he was a man of action and that she needed to put Haman in front of the king; and let it be known that Haman had vowed to kill Jews. It is obvious to me that Haman did not realize that Esther was a Jew. (Esther 7: 1-10) Queen Esther didn't use her beauty or female persuasion; she used her mind and the favor that was with her to position herself, the king and Haman in the same place at the same time.

Men, I need you to understand that we don't have to be perfect. The only perfect man is Jesus and even with our best days we fall short of His glory. However, we as men are commissioned to lead, to prosper as our soul shall prosper, and we are ear marked to perform to the best of our abilities in all that we do. We are designed with differences not perfections, but don't take imperfections to mean limitations. God created man to work and as I have stated before, the woman should help the man to achieve goals, plans and aspirations that will impact their life. Let me go a little deeper. The Proverbs 31 Man reads, "[11] her husband has full confidence in her and lacks nothing of value. [12] She brings him good, not harm, all the days of her life." One of the number one qualities that a man requires of a woman is TRUST. If we can trust you with our secret matters of our hearts, we will fight King Kong for you and win. Having full confidence in the woman in our life frees us and allows us to give unto her without a concern of feeling vulnerable. The woman is so valuable to us and the woman's gifts are immeasurable and the man lacks nothing with her in his life. With the freedom to love you the best way we know how and the willingness to learn more, there is no limit to what God would do with you and your relationship. There is so much that he would be willing to share with you. If a man has to guard his heart so much from you or from being hurt or made to feel belittled and insignificant, after a period of time he will not trust you. He will not communicate with you the way that you long for him to share. If your man can trust you with the smallest things on his mind, and also the largest mountain that he has to face, he will do whatever he can to make you feel special and appreciated. If you handle his heart and thoughts with tender loving care and patience, he will gain enough confidence in himself to succeed in those projects that are before him. Whatever project(s) he is facing, on his level, show him that you believe in him and he will love you for it. Communication is very important in any relationship and we must be willing to keep sharing as life challenges us in different areas. Over your lifetime you are going to loose friends, family members, money, gain money, your health will shift in different areas and you may not see each other the same, but you have to express your thoughts with the other person in order for them to keep up with you. In order to fulfill the purpose that God has placed on our life, we have to be honest with each other and continue to work at being with one another. We have to share our strengths and our weaknesses, for they are the natural things that make us who we are. Don't be ashamed or embarrassed because you don't do certain things better than someone else. Those other people that you may compare yourself with don't have your attributes either. You are the best you, you can be. No one on this planet can beat you being you. No matter how hard they try, you are uniquely designed and marvelously made. Your gifts and talents are like no other. So remember your value, your worth and know that the Lord is with you.

Unity

Ladies and Gentlemen, you need to realize that as a team working together and moving toward the same common goal, we can achieve so much more. From the beginning of Adam and Eve, I believe that it is God's orchestrated idea of men and women to jointly and equally work together in this lifetime. Remember we are made in His image and we are Sons and Daughters in the kingdom of God. We must learn together, help each other, encourage one another, and fight together against the enemy and the devils of this world. Unity is very important and we must not allow ourselves to be divided from each other. That's how the enemy easily comes in. No man or woman is an island. Ladies please understand what I'm saying. Yes, God has placed man as the head, but with equal submission. Man is subject to submit as well, but there is definitely a Devine headship that needs to be followed in order to receive the full measure of God's will and mantle of blessings. Men, when your lady knows a better way to do something or to take a better route on a trip, it's ok to listen to her. Stop acting like you know everything because you don't. And you know what men; it is ok when you don't have the answer. It's ok for her to do something or know something that you don't and you both are continuing to move toward that common goal. That is one of the ways that ladies fulfill the role as "help meet". Ladies let me help you out in another way. No matter how much he has achieved, no matter how many accolades that he has achieved, men need cheerleaders. We love it when you cheer us on. Men need to be made to feel like they are the King and you place no one else above them, besides God. Ladies when you show appreciation to your man and the more you celebrate him, he will take care of you even greater. He will make sure that you are made to feel special. He will make sure your needs are met. Now men, you deserve to be treated as Kings, but you need to display maturity and responsibility.

Life will bring you obstacles that will knock you down, but at some point and time, as a man you must stand upon your own two feet. Staying down is not an option. There are so many people counting on you. We all need one another to stand up and continue to press toward the mark of the high calling. Ezekiel 2:1 says, "And he said unto me, Son of man, stand upon thy feet, and I will speak unto thee." In order to be affective and productive we need to be standing uprightly and we need to be prepared and ready to listen to the instructions from the Lord to fulfill our next purpose. We are able to take on the next challenge when we know what's expected of us. We can lead boldly in the proper direction when we are clear in our thinking. For I know from great men and women before me that those who had much, did great things with little. Why is that? Because God blesses small numbers in order to show big harvests in Him. The Lord uses' large numbers and amounts as well, but His ability to use a remnant of people to conquer many, shows the greater power in God. Once you understand that God can use small beginnings, He is faithful to show up in that ugly situation and provide increase unto you in a bountiful way. However, your decision does have consequences. It would be irresponsible to walk out into the street and expel the Lord's blessings and protection on your life and think that you can not be hit. Do not temp the Lord thy God. He loves you, but He is nobody's puppet. Remember you will receive His protection, guidance, and prosperity when you are doing His will and you are fulfilling His purpose in your life. For our God would like all men and women to prosper.

Staying in God's will sometimes becomes a blur or confusing when we allow too many voices to enter into our minds and the best thing to do is to stop and ask for help. Women are better at dealing with their feelings and emotions than men. Men will try to continue to move forward when they are faced with a problem and will try to ignore it as long as they can, instead of dealing with it. Dealing with the issue, the problem, and the lack of finances is the huge elephant in the room that we keep talking around instead of taking the initiative to handle the elephant size problem, one issue at a time. Most of us find it humbling and difficult to cry out to God in times of trouble. We as men, ladies, prefer to be known as the strong, rugged, self-sufficient conquerors who can handle everything. We would rather endure pain, loose time and energy from a problem that is weighing on us with grave gravity. Yes, it's what we know as pride and egos. Here is a small and simple way to deal with an issue that you're faced with and you know that pride is in the way. You need to do what men and women have done throughout the scriptures in the bible. Take some time and find a nice quiet place and get alone with God and cry out to Him. Talk to Him, share with Him and He will give you the strength, the love and comfort you need so you can continue on the path that your feet are on.

Elderly Love

Let me share a true story in life that this young couple faced. We shall call them Robert and Regina. Robert's father had passed away and they felt that it would only be right and noble to take in his mother. His mother was much older than the young couple. The couple was twenty-three and twenty-four years old and his mother was sixty-seven. After a few years of living with them, his mother began knocking over things because her sight became slightly impaired and her hip was soar after falling a few times. Their house was decorated with fine china, and very exquisite vases that were on display and she accidentally knocked one over and broke it. Regina began to complain to Robert about his mother and she wanted to put her in a home for the elderly. Robert was against it at first until his mother broke a couple of bottles of aged and very expensive wine, which he would open for special guest in their home. The couple began to get very irritated with his mother and began making calls to find out where they could take her and they needed to know how much it was going to cost them. They found a couple of places that was very affordable and they felt that they could bring her there and not have to deal with here being a nescience to them anymore. After all, they felt like they have done their part of taking care of her for ten years. Well Robert and Regina was at a friends' house for dinner one evening and they began to share their happy plans for his mother.

They began sharing the tour of the facility where they had chosen and it did not sound very appealing. The building of this place was relatively small and it was not in the best shape. There was a maintenance man that was working on the gutters, replacing the fluorescent lights in the hallway and the elevator was out of service. The couple noticed that the walls were chipping from old paint and water damage that had stained the walls. There was this foul smell that came through the vents, but they thought that it was probably just a one-time thing. The place was not very staffed up, so the elderly guests were delayed care because of poor attendance for them. As they walked around the rooms, they noticed that the sheets were stained and it did not look as if they had been changed in weeks.

The friends interrupted them for a minute to say, Robert, this place does not sound very homey. This place does not sound very safe. This place does not sound as if there are activities that your mother would be able to participate in. Why would you want to send your mother in a place like this? Their friends also had a six year old daughter who was listening at the table. After she finished eating, she asked her parents, "may I be excused?" and she was free to go and play. The adults continued their conversation at the dinner table and then they noticed that their daughter brought in her giant dollhouse. She began bringing in the nice cars to play with and then she brings' in a small house. She goes and gets an old, beat up doll with hardly any cloths on and the cloths are dirty. From the conversation that she heard, she began to act out with her big beautiful house and fancy cars, what will happen to Robert's mother. Her father asked her what was she doing? The little girl said "daddy I'm just preparing a place for you and mommy when you get old". You are going to go to this little house and live, while I live in the big house and drive my fancy cars.

Needless to say, the couples just looked at each other with disturbed looks on their faces. The father asked Robert to rethink their decision because one day you will be old and your kids will be faced with making a decision about your life and well being. Robert and Regina drove home without saying a word on the entire drive home. When they arrived at home, they peeped in on his mother and she was sleeping on clean sheets and the room was secure without any bad smells. The look on his mother's face was very peaceful and sort of smiling. It was almost an angelic glow on her face. Robert and Regina went to their bedroom and started talking about a better resolution for his mother.

Robert and Regina calculated how much it would cost them to put his mother in an elderly home and decided that the money that they were going to spend would be better served in laser eye surgery for his mother. Not only that, but Robert decided that they would take her to the hospital and request a thorough examination with the medical insurance that she had. After careful diagnosis, his mother had hip surgery and she was walking much better, over time. Robert realized that the money that he and his wife accumulated and achieved was nothing without the love of his family. He had the revelation that making a living is not better than making a life.

Lord, thank you for wisdom, knowledge and the power to get wealth. For without You in our lives, life would be empty and not worth living. Dear Lord, You are our refuge and strength, and a very present help in trouble. Be Blessed.

Chapter 8

Lamb

Numbers 28:9
And on the Sabbath day two lambs of the first year without spot, and two tenth deals of flour for a meat offering, mingled with oil, and the drink offering thereof:

The Lamb was the sacrificial animal that was used to represent the type and shadow of the Lamb of God, Jesus Christ. The Lamb was used for sacrifices and it had to be a Lamb that had no physical defect. Our God's long-standing requirement is that we must offer our best to Him. Not that we should be perfect when we come to Him, but we should always give God our best. The Lord is called the "Lamb of God" throughout the Bible's Old and New Testament. This may seem to be a peculiar label to those who are not familiar with biblical idioms, but to those who know their Bible, it is a cherished title for our beloved, Jesus Christ. It is amazing to me that the almighty God, the majestic Omnipotent One, would come down from his thrown and take on the flesh and sins of the world, as an innocent lamb. In the book of John 1:29, John the Baptist's declaration of seeing Jesus for the first time was "Behold, The Lamb of God who takes away the sin of the world!"

In Exodus 12, you will find, probably the most compelling foreshadow of the coming Lamb of God. Moses and Aaron received the ordinance of the Passover from the Lord and would deliver this message to the people concerning the ordinance of the Passover. This new ordinance consisted of three parts. The first part was the killing and eating of the paschal lamb. You can find this in verse 1 through 6, and 8 through 11. The second part was the sprinkling of the blood upon the door-posts, spoken of as a distinct thing in Hebrews 11:28, and peculiar to the people of this first Passover. The third part was the feast of unleavened bread for seven days, which can be found in verses 14 through 20. Moses and Aaron were appointed by God to fulfill the instructions of the Passover. Understand that when you are called upon by God, you can achieve the most incredible task ahead of you. In spite of how difficult the task may be or how limited your ability is. The slain lamb was meant to be roasted and then eaten. The lamb, which represents the Lord, should be completely eaten by us, the believer. Our help and strength come from getting more of Jesus into us. Understand me, when I say eating the lamb, I'm talking about eating, (reading) God's word. That's how we get our strength and how we can communicate with God, but even better, God can communicate with us.

Before the people ate the flesh of the lamb, they were instructed to sprinkle the blood of the slain lamb upon the doorposts, verse 7. By performing this unorthodox process of making the houses distinguished from the houses of the Egyptians, this kept their first-born secured from the sword of the destroying death angel. Devastation was to be made that night in Egypt; all the first-born of both man and beast were to be slain, and judgment executed upon the gods of Egypt. It is important for you to understand the meaning and the gravity of the Passover and the Feast. The Passover Feast occurs each year on the fourteenth day of the Jewish month of Nisan. It is eaten today in remembrance of the Lord and the "passing over" of the houses of those who had sacrificed the Passover Lamb and sprinkled its blood on their wooden doorposts and mantles in Egypt. The angel of death was the final plague out of ten plagues, which was sent by God to redeem His people from slavery, out of bondage in Egypt. Approximately two thousand years ago, on the day of Nisan, the Passover Lamb of God, Jesus Christ, was sacrificed upon a wooden cross for the sins of all mankind. When the Day of the Lord comes, those who have covered themselves in the blood of the Lamb by accepting Christ will be kept safe while the world pays for their rebellion against God. History will repeat itself, in the since of another day of devastation to mankind.

Sacrifices

There is a sacrifice that we all must participate in throughout our lives. There is a biblical principal that is so true, the greater the harvest, the greater the sacrifice. The altar is a place of sacrifice. We should not approach the altar as a casual place to walk and talk. The altar is a place of reverence and respect. When Abraham prepared an altar to offer Isaac up to the Lord as a sacrifice, I promise you, Abraham did not take this command by God lightly. Remember this was Abraham and Sarah's first-born son, which was a blessing from God. The bible doesn't say this, but if it were my son that was asked of me to kill, I would beg the Lord to change His mind. My fatherly protection would kick in and my human sorrow would make it very difficult to fulfill the Lords request. However, Abraham believed that if God would take the life of his son, the Lord has the power to raise him up again. Abraham received the instructions and prepared Isaac and himself for the journey. The bible doesn't mention that he said too much to Sarah, but this was a divine request and unusual circumstances. This was going to be a father and son trip that no one would ever forget. Abraham, Isaac and two of his men arrived at the location and Abraham had the two men to wait at this spot afar off where God had shown him. Isaac was familiar with burnt offerings and he noticed that there was no lamb available. Abraham said to him with confidence, "the Lord shall provide Himself a lamb". The two of them arrived at the place for the sacrifice and Abraham placed the wood in its proper order. Abraham tied up Isaac and prepared to sacrifice his son. However, before Abraham could slay his child, God stopped his hand. Genesis 22:10-12 reads, "Abraham stretched out his hand and took the knife to slay his son. But the Angel of the LORD called to him from heaven and said, "Abraham, Abraham!" So he said, "Here I am." And He said, "do not lay your hand on the lad, or do anything to him; for now I know that you fear God, since you have not withheld your son, your only son, from Me". The Lord had prepared a ram in the thicket bush for Himself. Now before Abraham and Isaac would leave the mountain top where Isaac was to be offered as a sacrifice, Abraham again prophesies the coming of the Lamb of God, by saying in Genesis 22:14, and Abraham called the name of that place Jehovahjireh: as it is said to this day, In the mount of the LORD it shall be seen. Approximately 2,000 years later, upon that very same mountain just outside of Jerusalem, God offered His only Son, Jesus, the Lamb of God, as a sin offering to reconcile fallen man to the Holy Living God Almighty.

The Voice

Knowing that Jesus actually was beaten and died on a cross for me, for my sins, saddens me, encourages me, strengthens me, and ignites me to strive to live a better life. You have to know who you are in Christ and you have to know who Jesus is. Having a personal relationship with Jesus will keep you in line and in tune with His voice. You will know when you hear or see an unusual circumstance and it shall be revealed to you if it is of God or not. Try the spirit by the spirit. 1 John 4:1 "Beloved, believe not every spirit, but try the spirits whether they are of God: because many false prophets are gone out into the world." When John the Baptist was baptizing people in the name of Jesus, he knew the spirit of God. John baptized Jesus and he had no doubt that this was Jesus Christ, the Lamb of God. John witnessed for himself the Holy Spirit descending on Jesus and the Holy Spirit declared Him to be the Son of God. John knew that Jesus was the Christ, who had come to change the world and he knew that this was Jesus who had been prophesied in the book of Isaiah 53:7, " He was oppressed, and he was afflicted, yet he opened not his mouth: he is brought as a lamb to the slaughter, and as a sheep before her shearers is dumb [silent], so he openeth not his mouth."

Learning to trust the voice of God comes with being familiar with His word. Sometimes an unfamiliar spirit will come to tempt you and its' mission is to pull you away from your destiny and tries to get you to doubt the word of God. Sometimes the enemy will force you into a hard place or a confusing situation where you are not sure which way is right or wrong. When ever you come to this place, and trust me, just keep on living and one day you will; this place will give you a whole new perspective on life. Situations where you once valued and deemed important, will no longer hold the same value. Small issues seem to become big issues and our attention and value system gets revamped and we look at the major items as minimal importance now. It's not that the major issues are less important, we sometimes take our eyes off the true purpose of our endeavors and we allow the small issues to overwhelm us. When this happens, we tend to pay too much attention to the small, nagging issues that we need to deal with. Some small issues need immediate attention, but the enemy will send them to us just to be a distraction and deterrence. If the issues are really small we need to ignore it, bless it in Jesus name and move on. For example, when someone is talking about you or criticizing you behind your back, which is a small issue. Bless them and let them talk and keep going. You can't address every issue that you hear about. Although, I know you would like to, but it is not wise because you waste time and productivity towards your real purpose and goals. It may seem hard to do at times, but understand that these hard places or hard times will allow us to identify with the sufferings of others. Tough times for you prepares you and trains you to relate to those who you will come in contact with. It keeps us from having a shallow view of the hardships of others and allows us to truly identify with them. When you identify with the hurt and pain of others, you will be able to minister to them more affectively. Those who speak of such trials from no experience often judge others who have had such hardship. It is a superficiality of Christian experience that often permeates shallow believers.

Those who have walked in hard places immediately have a connection with others who have walked there also. Relating to that person and that situation and its' transparency quickly becomes identified. The individual that you are talking to does not need to explain a thing; they merely look at one another with mutual respect and admiration for their common experience. Also with mutual respect of one another, it is good to know that this person has your back. They are on your team with the same mindset and similar determination to complete a task at hand. It is impossible to really and truly appreciate any valley experience while you are in it. When you're in the valley place, you sometimes feel that you're the only one going through this and nobody understands your situation. However, once you have come out of the valley and you have reached the top of the mountain, you are able to appreciate what terrain you have passed through. You are able to look back and be in awe of where the Lord has brought you from. You may even marvel at what you were able to walk through and then realize that you are still here. The valley of the shadow of death has yielded more than you ever thought possible. You are able to appreciate the beauty of the experience and lay aside the sorrow and pain it may have produced. With this valley experience, we are able to humble ourselves and reach out to others and let that brother know that he is going to make it. He is coming out of this situation and we are going to shout and rejoice in Jesus name together. You will hug that sister and reassure her that the Lord has not forgotten where you are. For the Lord will never forsake you in good or bad times. He is true to His word and we must trust Him and know that everything will be all right. You will be able to say, “Hold on my sister”, “I have been there and he brought me out. I wanted to quit also, but He would not let me. He told me that I am wonderful and marvelously made, I am a queen and He is faithful to bring me out. I know that all this is for my good and I will be better in the end for this valley walk experience”.

Beloved, the Lamb of God knows your every thought and your every concern. The Lord wants me to tell you that everyone walking in the body of Christ is His’, and He is going to take all your valley experiences of insignificants to you and will make them significant breakthroughs for the kingdom of

God. To all my brothers and sisters in Christ, let me help you with some basic principals. When the Lord puts us in some of the most deplorable conditions and situations, and I know some of our situations look bleak and hopeless, but the deeper it seems we're going, the more that the Lord can move on your behalf. Trust me on this! God will get some glory out of your story! Hallelujah! It is God's spiritual character to turn the tables on the wicked ones. 1 Corinthians 4:10 says, "We are fools for Christ's sake, but you are wise in Christ; we are weak, but you are strong; you are honorable, but we are despised". The Lord relishes in the opportunity to show Himself strong for the weak, and it is his nature to confound the wise in this world's systems with foolish things. 1 Corinthians 1:27-28 says, "But God hath chosen the foolish things of the world to confound the wise; and God hath chosen the weak things of the world to confound the things which are mighty; And base things of the world, and things which are despised, hath God chosen, [yea], and things which are not, to bring to nought things that are".

Maturity

As the Lord encourages us to strive to be perfect, He does not say that so you can't make mistakes. The word perfect in the Greek means to mature, to make complete. The Lord finds pleasures in using the overlooked, the laughed at, the ostracized, because He knows how it feels to be that lamb that appears to be insignificant. The Lord knows when the saved or unsaved sees how the blessings have been poured into the once cast down lamb of the risen savior, those people will realize that it was no one but God who provided the way. So in the midst of your going through, know that your circumstances will bring God on the scene to show Himself strong in your situation. Your trials and tribulations are just setting the stage for your greatest miracle ever seen. The little lambs that have suffered with Him will reign with Him forever. So the next time you find yourself in the midst of a struggle, know that what the devil meant for evil, God will use the very same thing for your good. The Lord will work everything out.

Remember child of God, to use the tools that the Lord has given you. Speak the word, read your bible on a consistent basis. Don't just find the time to read, make the time to read. If there is a serious situation that that needs tending to, I know you will make the time to address that situation. The word of God is your strength, your way to fight the enemy back and to call upon the Lord who is a present help. In Hebrews 4:12 it says, for the word of GOD is quick, and powerful, and sharper than any two edged sword, piercing even to the dividing asunder of soul and spirit, and of the joints and marrow, and is a discerner of the thoughts and intents of the heart. The more you eat the word of God, the more you eat the Lamb of God, you will have a relationship that is closer to God and you shall retain power to fight off the enemy's tricks. It is human nature to think that you have achieved something on your own because all the ways of man are clean in his own eyes; but the LORD weighs the spirits.

You must give God all the praise and all the glory. You have to be prayerful and careful not to allow yourself to become proud in your heart. For the Lord hates a proud look. There is a way that seems right unto a man, but the end thereof is the ways of death. In 1 Samuel 16:7, "But the LORD said unto Samuel, Look not on his countenance, or on the height of his stature; because I have refused him: for the LORD seeth not as man seeth; for man looketh on the outward appearance, but the LORD looketh on the heart." What is in your heart today? Is there something that is causing you to be angry when you think on it? Do you see red when you hear a certain person's name? We must depend on the word of God to keep us from going into a state that will cause us to sin. For you have heard a preacher say that "man shall not live by bread only, but by every word that proceeds out of the mouth of GOD." Or " In the beginning was the word and the word was with GOD and the word was GOD." It is the word of God that changes your life. It is the word of God that will sustain you when your world feels as if it is coming down on you. The word of GOD will discern your thoughts and intents. We must try to keep a pure heart. If something wrong does creep into your heart, the word of God is like a two edge sword and will perform miraculous surgery on you. We often times say one thing with our mouths and then at the same time, speak or think something very different in our heart. The word of GOD discerns the heart. Your mouth will speak things that sound good, but your heart will not lie to God. God's word was made flesh and the word dwelt amongst us. The word is flesh in our heart and constantly discerns. The word allows us to have good judgment. If someone or something does not line up with the word of GOD when it is shared, then it will eventually be exposed, sifted, analyzed, and discovered that those very thoughts or words were not pure. Matthew 5:8 says it like this, “Blessed are the pure in heart for they shall see GOD.” People of GOD allow the word of GOD to sharpen, pierce, and discern your motives. Your motives are attached to your character, so improve them. You can build your character by consistently displaying integrity and humility to others. Showing love and doing what is right when no one is looking will build your character. When set out to do good toward your brother and sister, your motives and actions shows your humility to others. Commit thy works unto the LORD, and thy thoughts shall be established. In Proverbs 16:9 it states that “a man’s heart deviseth his way: but the LORD directeth his steps”. Humble yourself and come to the Lord as that little lamb and allow the word of GOD to discern your heart and I promise you shall have longer days of joy, long life of prosperity, and the peace of God that will be a treasure in your life.

Chapter 9

Leaders

Isaiah 55:4
Behold, I have given him for a witness to the people, a leader and commander to the people.

The ultimate example of a Leader is Jesus Christ. His lifestyle is the pattern and example that we all should be walking after. I'm not saying that we should be perfect; I'm saying that His walk is the example that is here for us to follow. When we think of leadership, we may picture our pastors helping us to stay on the right path, doctors taking care of their patients, lawyers standing in the court protecting their client, a military officer giving out orders or an employer closely supervising his employees, making sure all the work gets done. These aspects can be part of leadership, but this is not the only concept of leadership. In the home, the father is a leader and must show love, nurture and leadership to his family. You will need to teach as well as display positive leadership. The mother in the home has to show leadership as well. Mothers, regardless if you have kids or not, your actions is being peeped by someone and somewhere.

Let's begin the leadership actions with an affective prayer life. Luke 11:1 reads, "And it came to pass, that, as he was praying in a certain place, when he ceased, one of his disciples said unto him, Lord, teach us to pray, as John also taught his disciples". Do you understand its significance or power when you pray? The power of prayer has moved mountains, opened up the Red Sea, feed a multitude of people with two fish and five loaves of bread. The power of prayer has raised people from the dead, caused the sick to become healed, the blind to see, and the deaf to hear. There are a number of prayers and results of prayer in the Bible. There are also prayers for deliverance, for guidance, for forgiveness, for unity, and on and on. When you pray, it doesn't have to be this elegant, thunderous prayer to God. For prayer is your communication to our Father in Heaven. However, your prayers should be something or about someone that you have passion about. When someone says to you, "pray for me", that is your calling card to pray for them. Don't ignore it, because you never know what someone is going through. You should also learn scriptures to give you power and wisdom from the Lord. For the Lord shall teach you how to pray, also the Holy Spirit will as well. Your prayer time should become a time of intimacy between you and the Lord. When you pray more frequently, it will become such a habit that it will be second nature to you. You will be praying without ceasing before long. As you pray, take your time. You don't want to treat the Lord as if HE is a Burger King and you're placing and order to have your way. The Lord is our Father who enjoys our conversations and quiet time. He delights in you slowing down just to take some time to talk with Him and to listen to Him. Too many times people will pray and they will do all the talking, but will not stop long enough to listen to what God has to say. In this microwave world of ours, it's important that we slow down to hear from the master teacher. Now once you have done all of this, believe in what you've just prayed about. You must have the faith to believe that the Lord is able to fulfill what you have talked to Him about. Hebrews 11:1 states, "Now faith is the substance of things hoped for, the evidence of things not seen". When we pray sometimes, we expect results immediately. Sometimes God will reveal the answered prayers immediately and sometimes He will answer you in a way that you did not expect, but in God's timing. Unfortunately, we tend to keep doing what rewards us, so when prayer becomes an unrewarding experience we quit, we doubt, and we don't believe that God has heard our plea. He hears you, but as I have mentioned, it's in God timing. So, if you have thought along those lines, don't feel condemned about it. Develop your insight and become motivated to change your thinking and the way that you approach praying, for that's what being a leader is. Knowing how to switch and change from what he or she was doing, in order to get better results through growth in spiritual leadership.

Servant Hood

Leadership is not necessarily just being in charge. You have a responsibility to groom and nurture whomever is under your umbrella of guidance. Your development should be to motivate people and to build their self-esteem. You should be encouraging them to be the best that they can be. As a leader, you should be able to see certain attributes in people and note their strong points and their weak points and help them get better. Your heart and mindset should be as a servant. Jesus Christ Himself taught us, "just as the Son of Man did not come to be served, but to serve, and to give his life as a ransom for many" (Matthew 20:28). Spiritual leadership involves humbling yourself and doing the tasks that no one else wants to do. Again, I say unto you, Jesus is our ultimate teacher and example that has been displayed for our good. In John 13:12-17, it reads, "So after he had washed their feet, and had taken his garments, and was set down again, he said unto them, Know ye what I have done to you? You call me Master and Lord: and you say well; for so I am. If I then, your Lord and Master, have washed your feet; you also ought to wash one another's feet. For I have given you an example that you should do as I have done to you. Verily, verily, I say unto you, the servant is not greater than his lord; neither he that is sent greater than he that sent him. If you know these things, happy are you if you do them".

This display of humbleness, leadership and servant hood is such an example of love and care for your well being that it is done to love you. I have washed another persons' feet before and it has been done to me and it is such a humbling experience. You will have a completely different look on life when you have truly experienced the washing of someone's feet. Spiritual humility and a servant's heart will cause people to follow you because they want to, not because they have to. Genuine love and humility of spirituality can be felt and is attractive. People can feel that warm fuzzy feeling of love when you come around. People around the world, it doesn't matter what race, color or creed that they are, people will follow a person [leader], who serves alongside them and sets an example for them to follow. Even if they can't walk next to you, if they can hear you, praise God, if they can see you, they will follow and support your love, your vision as a leader and perform it well.

To be an effective leader, you need to put others before yourself. Please hear me, not to say that your duties or responsibilities are unimportant. What I'm saying is a good leader will be in the presents of people and make them feel that they are important, not the next meeting or event. I have experienced and I have heard of leaders that have met individuals and introduced themselves to them for a total of 10 seconds and they gave the impression that the person was the only one there for that moment. In my experience, their attention was focused purely on me and letting me know that it was a pleasure to meet me. Can you do that? Do you do that as a leader? If not, start talking to people with more concern and compassion. Allow them to see you and hear your heart. It will make the difference in their lives and with just a simple smile of acknowledgement; you can encourage someone to make better decisions in their life. Your leadership responsibility also requires you to have integrity. The word sounds good, but do you really know what it means? Integrity means to have a code of morals and ethics. Your actions are pure and honest. It's not hard to do, but you have to dismiss "pride". If you're not walking in integrity, start now. Ask the Lord for help and guidance and He shall provide it for you. It may come in the form of another person and if that's the case, humble yourself and listen to whom the Lord has sent to help you get where you need to be. Remember, that is what effective leaders do, they humble themselves and get better results from doing something in a different way. If people don't believe in you or respect you, they will not follow you.

Excellence

People will believe in you, as a leader, when you display the type of action that you would have them to do. If you want them to serve with a spirit of excellence, then you serve with a spirit of excellence. If you want them to show up to meetings on time and prepared for the meeting, then you need to show what you are asking of people. Ephesians 6:6-8 says it like this, "Not with eye service, as men pleasers; but as the servants of Christ, doing the will of God from the heart; with good will doing service, as to the Lord, and not to men: knowing that whatsoever good thing any man doeth, the same shall he receive of the Lord, whether [he be] bond or free". Your willingness to do unto others, as you would have them to do unto you is a golden rule that we all need to follow. Also, it is important to be honest. If there is something that you don't know or don't quite understand, it's ok to say, "I don't know the answer to that, but I will find out for you". Proverbs 16:13 teaches us, "Kings take pleasure in honest lips; they value a man who speaks the truth." Having solid values in your leadership skills and a wonderful spirit of humility and servitude will cause people to respond in a manner that they want to follow you. You may feel that you have to be stern, rough, and harsh in order for you to get a group of people to follow your instructions. Well in certain situations where you have to result to that because of the nature of the business, those actions may be warranted. However, in most cases, you don't need to go to those means. Being a drill sergeant, a coach, a correctional facility overseer, and I'm sure there are others that may use a more stern approach and voices that are yelling to get people to do what you're asking. The disrespect of others and their disobedience to follow the rules may force you to get them to do what you're asking. We all need discipline and it is the responsibility of the leader to be able to get his or her people to where they need to be. Spiritually leaders should not try to be drill sergeants and expect people to really listen, but on the other hand, spiritual leaders are coaches that teach people how to get out of that situation or circumstance and have a better life. We can help you to believe in yourself and give you the word of God that will give you the fresh anointing of hope. It was said of Moses, the leader of over one million Israelites, "Now Moses was a very meek [humble] man, more humble than anyone else on the face of the earth" (Numbers 12:3). Moses was an anointed leader and his spirit of humility was displayed wholeheartedly for everyone to witness and he served with excellence and determination.

Moses' powerful leadership was epic proof of results. He had solid support in brothers such as Joshua, Aaron and Caleb. These men were excellent leaders in their own right. The three of these men watched how Moses operated and they learned how to lead and how to depend on God. Just as the twelve disciples of Jesus, they were groomed to lead the people after God took their leader and teacher away. Jesus' work on earth was done and His teachings allowed His disciples to have over three thousand people to accept and believe the message of Jesus Christ on their first meeting. Acts 2:41 says, "Then they that gladly received his word were baptized: and the same day there were added unto them about three thousand souls". Powerful leadership will reproduce more of the same spirit and God will multiple the works even greater than what you had achieved. Jesus was one man, who took twelve men, taught them and discipled them to teach and preach the gospel and we have hundreds of millions of Christians today. All from Jesus, from the beginning, He set the precedence and the standards and over two thousand years later, He is still the number one teacher in the world.

Having an example that is laid out before you is such a benefit to your soul. The example of being a leader that is accountable is another attribute that is essential in your lifestyle that will help you to reach people. We are all held accountable in one-way or another in our life. Whether you really want to be accountable with your money, wife, husband, family, business or not, the Lord sets you up to be accountable. Let me put in layman terms as an example, there are laws in the land that we have to obey and if we fail to be obedient to them, we may have to suffer the consequences set by the authorities that be, who hold us accountable. Accountability is simply being responsible for one's actions. Being responsible for your own actions does not mean that you do things by yourself. No sir, No ma'am, you need others to be accountable to and to join with you in your journey. An effective leader needs the support and comfort of people who has the love, knowledge and wisdom of God, to show yourself approved unto others. As a leader you need to have people you can rely on and they need to be able to rely on you. When you have someone you can count on or rely on in the mist of a tough situation, this will allow you to build trust. To trust someone is a very important element in relationships, be it personal or business. It is important for every Believer to have at least one other person in which to confide, pray with, listen to, and encourage. You will need that someone in your time of a struggle or tight place. There are different things that can happen in life that will help you build trust if you don't have someone in your life that you can trust. The trials and tribulations in life are conditions that build you up, build your character and the people that are with you in these times will build trust amongst you. As people meet together to share, they begin to establish a rapport with one another. If you are going through an uncomfortable time in your life, where you are experience some embarrassing moments, it's a time that you are going through some down time while the Lord is giving you time of preparation. Don't allow yourself to stay in anger. Don't allow your thoughts to wander into frustration and you cannot hear what your help is trying to share with you. James 1:19 says, "My dear brothers, take note of this: Everyone should be quick to listen, slow to speak and slow to become angry." As a leader, your ability to listen with the quickness shows your obedience to the word of God. Your true hearing of God's word is more than just listening. God's word in your life must be received by you and then actively applied in your life. That means that when things are not going the way that it should be going for you at that time, continue to show love. Check your attitude and open up yourself up to others that you have established trust with and share what is bothering you. Share with them how you feel and allow them to have some personal information about yourself. People who relate to one another can empathize and share with an understanding heart. People can feel comfortable in sharing their circumstances, and can be totally accepted without fear of rejection. Get this scripture in your spirit; it will help to keep you from jumping to conclusions about others and their circumstances. In Matthew 7:1-2 says, "Do not judge, or you too will be judged. For in the same way you judge others, you will be judged, and with the measure you use, it will be measured to you." Your responsibility as a Christian does not mean that we are to close our eyes to the wrong character of people, but we are to hold a standard of accountability that should be followed. However, as Christians, we should not be so critical of others and we should not be faultfinders in others. Love them with the spirit of God and lead them where the Lord is leading you. When you are pressed on every side, sometimes you are not sure which direction to turn. It may seem cloudy in the beginning, but remember the voice of the Lord who spoke into your destiny and not the voice of one's circumstances! You will never have a lack of people to preach to, build up, lead into championships, and break financial goals, when you meet people's needs. In Psalm 16:8, I have set the Lord always before me. Because he is at my right hand, I will not be shaken. There are many things that can trouble our lives, but none that can shake us loose from the grip of God's grace if our hearts remain close to Jesus as our Lord and personal savior, and our hope remains focused on the Lord's return. As we work until the return of our risen savior, I admonish you that you stay close to the Lord's word and if someone is caught in a sin, you who are spiritual should restore him gently. But watch yourself my brothers and sisters, for you also may be tempted. Yes, you are my brothers' keeper and we are to help each other when challenged with burdens, and in this way you will fulfill the law of Christ. It is still imperative that we cast our cares, hurts and burdens on the Lord. For the Lord is the burden removing, yoke destroying and the all-powerful one. For He shall provide us with complete comfort and directions in our times of need. For those of you who may be wondering where your spiritual level of leadership may be on the spiritual radar. I will define it in this like manner of David, whom I love. You will know that you are in the realm of being a highly anointed leader by the level of attacks you encounter. The roar of lions or the cheering of the crowd, will not measure true anointing in your life. It will be the number of javelins that are thrown at you! But remember, "No weapon formed against you shall prosper", Hallelujah!

Chapter 10

Liberty

Romans 8:21
Because the creature itself also shall be delivered from the bondage of corruption into the glorious liberty of the children of God.

The truth in life regarding liberty is our right of freedom. It is a privilege and a luxury to have freedom, when there are still people living in bondage. Webster's Dictionary explanation of the word "Liberty" is the freedom from slavery or captivity. 2) A particular right or freedom. 3) A pertinent attitude. I thank God that we live in a country that we can call the "Home of the free and the Home of Liberty". From a Christian stance, 2 Corinthians 3:17 states, "Where the Spirit of the Lord is, there is liberty." America is a country that the Lord has His hand on and the people in this country recognizes the privilege and freedom to love one another, freedom to own your own home, own your own business, and worship how you see fit. We're not in a country where you would be killed for saying Jesus. We're not in a country where you cannot read the bible. We have the liberty to choose which bible translation we would like to read today. We can switch and read another translation tomorrow. No one in America has revoked our rights to read what we choose to read.

About two years ago, I went to Philadelphia on a business trip and I had some extra time on my hands, so I decided to explore the city. One of the exhibits that I wanted to see was the world famous LIBERTY BELL, at the Liberty Bell Center. The first thing that I noticed was the statement, "Let Freedom Ring". There were statues and information displays explaining the national celebration and the reasons for honoring everyone involved with achieving America's independence during the American Revolution. I read another display of America's president in 1969; Richard W. Thorington, at that time, he said "Let Freedom Ring, in order to revive the spirit of patriotism." This speech was to give hope to millions of Americans that we will be free to function as an independent country and the government would not allow anyone to infringe on our rights of freedom. I also read that on July 8, 1776, Colonel John Nixon had the Liberty Bell ring to summon the citizens to hear the first public reading of the Declaration of Independence. Our rights and freedom were in jeopardy and America's religious freedom as well. To my surprise, there was a bible scripture that was quoted in order to support the fight for liberty. The bible scripture that was used was Leviticus 25:10, "And ye shall hallow the fiftieth year, and proclaim liberty throughout [all] the land unto all the inhabitants thereof: it shall be a jubilee unto you; and ye shall return every man unto his possession, and ye shall return every man unto his family." I thought that was interesting and good for the people to know their freedom of liberty was very important. The visit to see for myself the Liberty Bell and its artifacts gave me more of a sense of appreciation for liberty. Our American government was fighting another country to protect our liberty rights to be free. Our government was fighting to keep us out of bondage.

Bondage

Bondage began with Adam receiving and eating the fruit in the Garden of Eden. In one act, in one instance, the door of disobedience and sin entered into their world as Adam and Eve knew it. I am sure Adam wished he had that moment back in time. There is no doubt in my mind that Adam realized and felt the horrible stench of sin. Until the eating of the fruit by Adam, he was normally innocent. However, the devil wastes no time in letting Adam, or you and I know that we have sinned and have made a terrible mistake. Adam and Eve had two sons, Cain and Abel. Now sin is made even more evident when Cain kills Abel. Genesis 4:8, "And Cain talked with Abel his brother, and it came to pass when they were in the field, that Cain rose up against Abel his brother, and slew him." The selfishness, hatred, bitterness and anger originated within Cain because of the sin inside of him. Because of his sin, Cain was punished to till the ground and to become a vagabond on the earth. (Genesis 4:12)

The children of Israel were in bondage of Pharaoh for years, but the entire redemptive time was about 430 years. The Lord told Moses that HE would bring them out of bondage from the Egyptians. The Lord would rescue them and redeem them with an out stretched arm and with great judgments. (Exodus 6:6) Moses was not confident in himself or with what the Lord promised him. As we all do sometimes, we look at the situation and circumstances with our own eyes and we fail to hear what the Lord had shared with us. The Lord shared with Moses his duty to face Pharaoh and to lead the people out of bondage, and Moses would do this by the strong hand of God's grace. For the Lord has a strong hand of power, and some may feel his strong hand of justice because of disobedience, this hand of justice will be the breaking of those who would not bend. After ten plagues that were released upon Egypt and Pharaoh's household. The death angel had passed at midnight and all of the firstborn were struck dead. Even the firstborn of cattle and livestock were slain. Pharaoh finally called for Moses and released the people from bondage. Exodus 12:31, "And he called for Moses and Aaron by night, and said, Rise up, and get you forth from among my people, both you and the children of Israel; and go, serve the LORD, as you have said."

The Lord has freed us from the snares of bondage. However, there are places where people are afraid to speak up for themselves as men and women. Some of the women have to stay positioned in a posture that is lower than a man. In some parts of the world, men and women still have no will or say so of their own. These people have no principles, no voice, no courage, and they cannot stand erect in conscious independence. If they attempt to do so, the consequences could be imprisonment, torture, or even death. I thank God that Jesus broke the curse of bondage way back on Calvary. Because of Christ, I walk, live and breathe the Spirit of the

Lord, and the Lord is liberty. The Lord has made us free from the bondage of sin. Romans 8:1-2 reads, "There is therefore now no condemnation to them which are in Christ Jesus, who walk not after the flesh, but after the Spirit. For the law of the Spirit of life in Christ Jesus hath made me free from the law of sin and death." To live as an unbeliever is a miserable place. You think that you're having fun and everything is "all good", but you're fooled, you're sadly mistaken. Of all the bondage and slavery that has taken place and is still taking place today, to live in that state is such a horrible condition. My brothers and sisters, for those who have not received the Lord as their personal savior, you are living in the bondage of sin. To walk around in life with the weight of sin on your shoulders is a burden that is too heavy for anyone to carry. That's why it is a joy and privilege to walk in the freedom of Christ. Christians will walk around smiling, signing and sometimes laughing amongst themselves and you may wonder why. Let me help you get the revelation. It is the Liberty of walking with Jesus. As Christians, we have the Liberty to sing a song and make a joyful noise from our hearts.

Patriotism

On March 23, 1775, *Patrick Henry* gave a famous speech called, “Give Me Liberty Or Give Me Death”. I thought it would be good for you to read just a little of his speech.

"No man thinks more highly than I do of the patriotism, as well as abilities, of the very worthy gentlemen who have just addressed the House. But different men often see the same subject in different lights; and, therefore, I hope it will not be thought disrespectful to those gentlemen if, entertaining as I do opinions of a character very opposite to theirs, I shall speak forth my sentiments freely and without reserve. This is no time for ceremony. The questing before the House is one of an awful moment to this country. For my own part, I consider it as nothing less than a question of freedom or slavery; and in proportion to the magnitude of the subject ought to be the freedom of the debate. It is only in this way that we can hope to arrive at truth, and fulfill the great responsibility, which we hold to God and our country. Should I keep back my opinions at such a time, through fear of giving offense, I should consider

myself as guilty of treason towards my country, and of an act of disloyalty toward the Majesty of Heaven, which I revere above all earthly kings.

Mr. President, it is natural of man to indulge in the illusions of hope. We are apt to shut our eyes against a painful truth, and listen to the song of that siren till she transforms us into beasts. Is this the part of wise men, engaged in a great and arduous struggle for liberty? Are we disposed to be of the number of those who, having eyes, see not, and, having ears, hear not, the things which so nearly concern their temporal salvation?

It is in vain, sir, to extenuate the matter. Gentlemen may cry, Peace, Peace-- but there is no peace. The war is actually begun! The next gale that sweeps from the north will bring to our ears the clash of resounding arms! Our brethren are already in the field! Why stand we here idle? What is it that gentlemen wish? What would they have? Is life so dear, or peace so sweet, as to be purchased at the price of chains and slavery? Forbid it, Almighty God! I know not what course others may take; but as for me, give me liberty or give me death!" By Jawaid Bazyar.

This speech by Patrick Henry was very powerful and also precarious speech for the time that he spoke this. Our country was at war and the words that he used to address the President of the United States were very directive and he stood boldly to stand and declare that he respected and reverence. However, the freedom of speech and the liberty of this country, allows us the freedom to speak as American citizens. It is everyone's responsibility not to abuse God, our country and our liberty that we have been given. Satan will try to take it away, men and women will try to take it away, other countries will try to take it away and we have to stand for righteousness sake and fight to keep what is rightfully ours. Ephesians 6:11 "Put on the whole armor of God, that you may be able to stand against the wiles of the devil". Let's pay attention to the words ... "that you may be able to stand." We as Christians have to be reminded sometimes that in those hard times and tough times and those times that we have to fight; we must stand. It will help you if you understand that the battle is not yours, it is God's and guess what, the armor that you put on is God's. The Lord is asking you to do your part and your part is to stand! The power of liberty is from God and HE expects you to fight with His armor. God's armor is for those who are willing to stand for what's important; for example, when the enemy comes after the salvation of your family, or the enemy attacks the success of your marriage. The enemy will attack what ever you deem as important to you. The enemy will attack your friends, your church, your finances, your health, your walk with God, and anything else that's of value to you. Beloved let me be very clear; you must suit up, strap up and stand up and hold your ground! For the enemy comes in to steal, kill and to destroy. Do not fret and do not fear, our Lord has our back, our front and HE has us covered all the way around.

Not Forgotten

It is so important to remember or to be reminded that Jesus is the truth and the life and He has broken the hand that holds anyone to sin. That hand has been given to all in the liberty of love from our wonderful, sweet savior Jesus Christ. I have to keep saying it because He has done all there is to be done, and we just have to believe in Him and accept the Lord. That wicked hand of Satan produces schemes and tricks to make Believers think that the Lord has forgotten about them. The Lord has not forgotten about you. He loves you and He knows exactly where you are. It may seem as if you're all alone or have been forgotten when the difficulties of life smacks' you in your face. The Lord allows certain trials and tribulations to come upon us to strengthen us and prepare us for acquisitions of new positions that are in line with your purpose. James 1:2-4 reads, "James, a servant of God and of the Lord Jesus Christ, to the twelve tribes which are scattered abroad, greeting. My brethren, count it all joy when ye fall into divers temptations; Knowing [this], that the trying of your faith worketh patience. But let patience have [her] perfect work, that ye may be perfect and entire, wanting nothing."

When life gets confusing, stressful, or even tragic, you may wonder if God sees or cares about you. God knows your thoughts and He knows when your faith is starting to waiver. He will answer your prayer in His timing and your life will be changed for the better. God will give you personal touches to show you His love, and to show you His sovereignty. God enjoys loving you; He sends love with a wink to you as from a loving Father who wants you to know He's watching over you. God has always performed extraordinary miracles through people who appeared to be ordinary people with little or no avenues of a way out. Pay close attention to how God may choose to validate His presence through any situation in your life. Understand that God reveals Himself not just in momentous, astronomical events, but also in small, mundane moments that will mean so much in your life. God will answer a prayer that only you and He talked about and when it happens, your heart is filled with joy. It is filled with joy because you know that He is with you. You have received concrete evidence that God is with you and He is still faithful in your life.

Satan wants people to believe a lie and that our suffering is in vain. Satan wants us to believe that our following Christ is foolishness and Christ is not faithful in His word. Satan wants you to believe in his word and persuade you to leave the righteousness and covering of Christ and cleave to the basket of emptiness and destruction. This sloth foot devil wants you to walk in fear and wander this world without hope. My brothers and sisters I write to you now to speak hope into your lives. I prophesy that your greater days are in front of you and your life will have an evolutionary change of spiritual gratification. Your hopes and dreams shall come to pass, according to the purpose and plans for your life, deemed by Jesus. I bind those ill-gotten thoughts and those negative clouds of stress and unfulfilling plans in the name of Jesus. Satan has no place in your life. He can only deceive you into going into that dark hole of sin. Do not focus on the circumstance that you are faced with. The Lord is true and faithful to His word. The

Lord cannot deny His own word and faithfulness to His word. 2 Timothy 2:13 says, "If we believe not, yet he abideth faithful: he cannot deny himself."

Promise

The Lord has given Christians the promise of His love, His word and eternal life for Believers. The liberty of God's love is to save you from the deceptions of the enemy. Unfortunately, sometimes Christians will doubt God's love and presence simply because they do not feel Him near or because of the disturbances around them. Since the beginning of time, God had us in mind and His word states that He promised to graciously accept us, through Jesus Christ (Titus 1:2) "In hope of eternal life, which God, that cannot lie, promised before the world began." With this promise from God, I admonish you to walk in the grace of God and expect an abundant life. (John 10:10) "The thief cometh not, but for to steal, and to kill, and to destroy: I am come that they might have life, and that they might have [it] more abundantly." When Satan whispers foolish thoughts of you not being important or that you won't achieve that degree, or you won't get that house or car, or you won't get that promotion, you just remind him that you are the Lord's child. You remind him that the Lord has sealed you with a promise for your present well being, your future well being and your final destiny in heaven is where your liberty of life shall permanently dwell.

The Lord has given His liberty of love to the entire world to receive, but everyone is not His children. The Lord will speak to His children and His children know His voice. John 10:3-5, "To Him the porter openeth; and the sheep hear His voice: and He calleth his own sheep by name, and leadeth them out. And when He putteth forth his own sheep, He goeth before them, and the sheep follow Him: for they know His voice. And a stranger will they not follow, but will flee from him: for they know not the voice of strangers." The Lord will speak to His children in many different ways. The Lord spoke to Moses through a fiery bush on the mountain top. The Lord spoke through a donkey to Balaam on the road, while an angel of the Lord stood in the road with a sword. The Lord spoke through prophets to His Kings. The Lord speaks to us through the comforter, the Holy Spirit. Whenever He deems it necessary, He will speak directly to us without any interference from outsiders, busy schedules or projects that are important to you. The Lord will bring you to a place of quietness and to a calm state of mind. When the Lord is speaking to you in this place, you do not want to be distracted. It is your best interest to properly take some time to hear from the Lord, before disaster strikes you. Unfortunately, we sometimes get pushed into that prayer time with the Lord. We get pushed in because we do not keep a regular dialogue with Him as we should. When the issue of life hits us while we are talking to Him, He is faithful to prepare us and He will walk us through whatever life brings our way. With our busy lives of tasks, memos, meetings and appointments, we will discover in the moment of calamity that the Lord has been with us all the time. When we are so busy with life, we sometimes forget that the Lord's hand is gently leading us and guiding us along the path in which we should go. The Lord has spoken to me sometimes and I heard Him, but did not follow His complete instructions. Because I was busy with my daily functions and tasks on my to-do list, He had to gently turn my head in the direction that He told me to go. He had to take more drastic measures to get my attention. There was this time where the Lord specifically spoke to my spirit and shared with me that He wanted me to spend some quality time with Him for lunch time at work. I heard His voice and I prepared myself by bring my bible with me and I had my notebook and pen. When the appointed time came for me to take that time to read the word, some co-workers asked me to go to lunch with them. They kept asking and pushing and I knew what I needed to do, but I went to lunch with the guys. This was a good idea, but it was not a God idea. I knew what the Lord had said to me, but I allowed peer pressure of being with the group persuade me into joining them for lunch instead of spending that quality time with the Lord, needless to say, I did not have a good lunch. My spirit was troubled and I was very uncomfortable. Everyone else was having a good time, but I was not. That night, the Lord woke me up at 3:00 am and said to me "I asked you for quality time, not rushed time. Now you are going to spend this time with me." The time spent with the Lord was refreshing, nourishing and I was aspired with new revelation. This time with the Lord should have taken place when I heard from the Lord and agreed to the time. My spirit was not settled because I was disobedient with a simple time agreement that I made with the Lord. However, because of the love and liberty that the Lord freely gives us, He continues to faithfully keep us on track. That does not give anyone a license to just to do whatever you want and expect to be rectified later. No, because you will have consequences to deal with for any disobedience and you do not want to go through any persecution that you bring upon yourself. Because Satan will have you dabble into sin longer than you want to be there and he will have you go further than you wanted to travel. He will have you so deep into trouble without you even realizing that. However, the Lord is our Savior, our hope, our strength that rescue's us out of all iniquity. The Lord is our fortress, our help in the presence of our enemies, and our wheel in the middle of a wheel. Thank you God; for the Liberty of your salvation; thank you for the love from your heart; and best of all, thank you for your son and our Lord, Jesus Christ.

Chapter 11

Lion

Revelation 5:5
And one of the elders said unto me, weep not: behold, the Lion of the tribe of Judah, the Root of David, hath prevailed to open the book, and to loose the seven seals thereof.

Oh mighty lion, we hear your roar as you walk amongst the land, we thank of ourselves as being safe within your hand. Your mane is beautiful and full with shape and body that everyone admires. With hope, faith, goodness and aspirations, we are blessed with the desires of our hearts because you bless us through our dedications. You are by nature wild and men try to tame, but the main voice that captures your attention is the one we call in Jesus name. You are strong and mighty, you are fierce and brave and your very presence proclaims that you are, I Am. Many tremble because of your power, but your approach is as gentle as a lamb. Oh Lord and Savior! How amazing is your wonderful love and care, the angels on high expresses in song as the melodies carries us there. We know in which our help cometh and we shout it on the mountain tops that everyone should proclaim, when you are in any type of crisis, call on Jesus name.

This is a poem that the Holy Spirit gave me as I began this chapter. I believe that it was given to me to share with everyone because no matter whom you are or when you need Him, the Lord is always there with us. Most Christians that has followed the Lord's teaching over a number of years have seen Him perform miracles and blessings in our modern day and times that has continued to captivate us. When you have seen and experienced miracles for yourself, you tend to expect to see them even more. Whenever I have been blessed to witness God's Glory, I have a greater desire to know His will and purpose for my life. My desire is to be the best man of God, man of valor, man of substance that I can be. As I have walked this life as a man that is seeking God's heart, I have made some mistakes, I have faulted along the wrong path, but God has sustained me and have ordered my steps to get back in line. Just like when your father or mother corrects you as a child. If I was doing the wrong thing or saying the wrong thing, my parents would get that belt and correct my ways and help me to get back in line. You know what I'm talking about. My parents believed in the scripture of not sparing the rod and showed me that they loved me by correcting my actions. When I would disappoint my parents with making the wrong decision, they did not enjoy spanking or punishing me for my actions. However, they had given me their rules about not staying out too late or not to repeat what I heard other kids say that was not appropriate. My parents would tell something like, "Jr., do not let those streetlights catch you". You may have heard that "*Hope deferred makes the heart sick.*" When I did something that made my parents heart a little sorrowful, it didn't mean that they did not love me, but only that they are sorry that I didn't learn from my mistake from the previous encounter.

Valor

Learning how to behave myself and conduct myself as the mighty Lion of Judah, my quest has been to reside as a mighty man of valor. So what does it mean to be a "Mighty Man of Valor?" You may be asking yourself am I one? What does it take to be one? Well, Webster's dictionary version of this is to be strong or to show courage and bravery. Now women are strong and have shown courage and bravery throughout history. So I don't want to loose the women in thinking that this is for the men only. No dear lady, I hope that you can get a better understanding of what men should be standing as and also, allowing you to look into the development of the man or young man in your life. It is a wonderful thing to know God as your Lord and as your leader. As men, we try to stand strong and we don't want you to see us in a vulnerable state or to appear weak in a moment of stress. So we try to look strong even when we are beat down. We look to God for our strength and for Him to redeem us as we follow Him. The enemy knows that we as men take it really hard when we don't make enough money or a business decision goes bad. The truth of it is that money is "power". The Lord gives us power to get wealth because we need money to operate in this world we live in and He wants us to live the abundant life. When a man is thrown in a pit of lack or a den of low finances, his self-esteem is brought low as well. It takes a lot of fighting within to not stay there. If you're married and have kids, you're concerned that you're not going to be able to take care of your family. You would find yourself asking, "How am I going to feed my family?" "How am I going to pay these bills?" If you are single, you want to be able to take care of yourself. As a man, you don't want to have to borrow from someone or promise to pay someone back if they are willing to help you out of a jam. Being strong and courageous as a "Mighty Man of Valor" does not seem to be happening to you in this situation, but God has a way of using your situation to show Himself strong and mighty through you. God is always teaching us and will bring you out of any situation or circumstance that the enemy has set you up in. No matter what type of pit the enemy has thrown you into, your God is well able to deliver you out of it. Furthermore, no matter what type of spiritual lion is threatening to consume you today, God can shut its mouth. Just like He shut the lions' mouth in (Daniel 6:16-22) for Daniel. He was a "Mighty Man of Valor" even though his circumstances did not show that at that time. Bankruptcy or some other type of financial peril is threatening some of you. Others of you feel like you are being eaten alive by the sin preying on your soul. Be encouraged my brothers in sisters, whatever mountain of despair that you may be facing today, the same God who sent His angel to shut the lions' mouths for Daniel, is with you today. It doesn't even matter if you have never seen or heard of another Christian who has been delivered from what you are facing.

In 1 Corinthians 10:13, God promises to always provide us with a way of escape. It reads, "No temptation has overtaken you except such as is common to man, but God is faithful, who will not allow you to be tempted beyond what you are able, but with the temptation will also make the way of escape, that you may be able to bear it." You will be delivered and once you are, you may continue to receive a few phone calls from bill collectors or others issues that have not been settle yet, but give it some time. Even Daniel had to spend the night in the lion's den. Remember, God is always teaching us and you have been brought out of the lion's den, but there may be some repercussions that you may have to endure. God may merely be testing your faith to show you where you are and you must continue to seek Him. In seeking Him, you have to decide where you're going. You, as a mighty lion, must develop a plan that will guide you and help you attain your goals.

Vision

Make positive, attainable goals in your life. In Habakkuk 2:2, God to the prophet to "write the vision and make it plain on tablets, that he may run who reads it." Understand that if you do not have goals and something to strive for, you are working as a faulty compass. You have no direction or you go in the wrong direction. Your compass of life is off and you can easily be swept off course that God has planned for you. Yes, God will fulfill His purpose for your life, but you don't want to have to stumble and fall unnecessarily. A wise lion will be watchful of his surroundings and when God sends some help, he or she will be able to receive what God has in store for them. God will reveal His plan for your life if you continue to seek him. When a lion is hungry, he will roam the land until he sees his prey before him. The lion will strategize and hunt to get what he needs to fulfill his destiny.

Let me tell you another true story about a strong and courageous woman by the name of Helen Keller. At the tender, developing age of 19 months old, Helen Keller contracted the illness that eventually left her without hearing and sight. In the 1800's, you were labeled "deaf and dumb" and you were classified as an idiot if you had these abnormalities. Helen had strong parents who did not receive the comments of the people. So, her parents hired a private teacher by the name of Anne Sullivan to work with their daughter. After a period of time, Helen learned how to read and write by using Braille.

What a remarkable achievement so her parents thought. However, God was not through with Helen yet. Amazingly enough, Helen graduated in 1904 with honors from Radcliffe College. Helen knew that God had blessed her to achieve such greatness and she knew she had a purpose and responsibility in her life. Helen began to help others who had her same personal afflictions. Helen had done so well that Philanthropist Andrew Carnegie paid her an annual salary to continue her work. Helen's work spread so much that even writers such as Mark Twain and Robert Louis Stevenson praised her for such courageous achievements. It is respectfully noted that several Presidents of Helen's day, invited her to our illustrious White House in Washington, D.C. Helen died in 1968, but her legacy of courage and bravery lives on strong today. Before Helen passed away, someone asked her if there was anything worse than being blind, remarkably Helen replied, "Yes, having sight but no vision."

Another story of heroism was the little boy who was twelve years old who suffered with a severe case of hearing loss. This little boy was Thomas Edison. His hearing was so bad that his teachers recommended that he be taken out of school and taught from home. The teachers didn't have the time to spend with Thomas to give him extra attention. Thomas Edison began to use his hearing handicap to drown out distractions and focus more on his work. As a result of this, the boy who was labeled "a distraction and a slow learner" did very well with his education. This "slow learner" gave our world over one thousand inventions in his lifetime. You know some of them, like the light bulb, the phonograph and the motion picture camera. Whether these two amazing people realized it or not, but God instilled into them the courage of a lion. They over came obstacles with the bravery of their souls, their minds and the guidance of the Lord.

Bravery

There are many biblical stories that show bravery and courage as well. Bravery was shown when Abraham was told to leave his fatherland in Genesis 12:1-9. It took courage and faith for Abraham to offer up his only son for a sacrifice in Genesis 22:1-14. The fearless leader of Deborah, the prophetess, in Judges 4; where she was commanded by the Lord to lead the children of Israel. How about being asked to take an entire nation of people from a commander and chief of Egypt, there is no doubt in my mind that Moses needed encouragement. God called Moses to a position of leadership and to walk with courage. I encourage you to read Exodus 3:1-22, in order to see how it was a little disheartening for Moses to do what God had asked of him. Have you ever thought about how Moses felt after he murdered an Egyptian and, fearing for his life, Moses fled into the wilderness? For forty years Moses lived in the desert, undoubtedly hounded by a host of condemning voices. So when God appeared to him in the burning bush, Moses was struggling with past sins, self doubt, and the result of failure and rejection. God would simply say to Moses, "I will be with you." Above all, Moses needed God's reassuring presence. Without Him, Moses could never stand before Pharaoh; left alone, he would certainly fail.

Rather than focusing on God, Moses focused on himself. He was like the little boy in the school play whose one line was, "It is I, be not afraid." But on the night of the play, the boy came out on stage and exclaimed, "It's me, and I'm scared!" Please notice that in this chapter of Moses' life, part of God's solution to Moses' crisis of confidence was a companion, which God gave him Aaron. The two brothers became a team. Undoubtedly, Aaron frequently reminded Moses of the truth.

The truth was that Moses was God's man for the assignment, and God would be faithful to His promises.

Moses did not mean to be objective, but I'm sure he didn't understand how God could talk to him through a bush of flaming fire either. Moses believed that God is God, but "who am I" to do such great work in Egypt. Moses thought only in the term of his own resources when God challenged him to perform this mighty task. Moses thought of his stuttering, and he wondered if God's power would be enough to free the people. It is one thing to hear a command, but Moses wondered if God would be with him when he addressed Pharaoh. I definitely understand why Moses would be hesitant and asking such proverbial questions. However, the obviously truthful questions that Moses was asking were rational and logical in this matter. I understand from my own struggles why Moses would ask the question, "Who am I?" but Moses should have asked, "Whose am I?" In remembering whose you are, brings back fortitude and reassurance of your place with the Lion of Judah.

Joshua

I love the characters of Joshua and David also because I can relate to them in my own personal life. It took an extremely large amount of strength, courage, faith and dedication to God's word to stand with the heart of a lion and move when God said to move. Joshua's life is parallel with the life of Jesus Christ, for his name is Yeshua, which means Yahweh is salvation. This name is the Hebrew name that is equivalent to Jesus. Joshua was commissioned also to triumphantly lead God's people into a land of possessions. Now thanks be unto God, who always leads His people to victory. Although, Joshua was a little nervous, just as I am when God ask me to do something. It is comforting to know that the Lord will encourage us and allow our leadership to grow, just as he did Joshua when he asked him to go over Jordan. The Lord told him that He is giving him this land and in Joshua 1:3 he said, "Every place that the sole of your foot will tread upon I have given you, as I said to Moses." In verse 5, the Lord had to encourage him and remind him that He would be with him just as He was with Moses. The Lord said to Joshua that, "I will be with you. I will not leave you nor forsake you." Because God made us and He knows us better than we know ourselves, He knows just what to do and just what to say for us to be where we're supposed to be and get what we're supposed to have. The Lord said to Joshua in 1:7-8, "Only be thou strong and very courageous, that thou mayest observe to do according to all the law, which Moses my servant commanded thee: turn not from it to the right hand or to the left, that thou mayest prosper whithersoever thou goest. This book of the law shall not depart out of thy mouth; but thou shalt meditate therein day and night, that thou mayest observe to do according to all that is written therein: for then thou shalt make thy way prosperous, and then thou shalt have good success." Remember that Joshua had just succeeded Moses in the leadership of the nation Israel. Moses had led the nation for forty years and was reared in the household of the king. Moses was seasoned and he walked closely with God. Joshua would ask himself, "How am I going to follow after such a great man as Moses?" Joshua new that he had not seen the things that Moses saw or done even half the things that Moses achieved. Joshua was put in a place that he had no experience in doing. He had the awesome responsibility of commanding two and a half million people across the Jordan. Lord have mercy. Do you know how many personalities that he had to get in line to follow his leadership? If there was anyone who needed encouragement, it was Joshua. His heart must have rested with gladness and assurance whenever he heard the Lords voice of comfort and instruction.

David

It is always a privilege and an honor to serve God's people and to be charged with a specific duty by God. When God anoints you to perform a specific task, you begin to work in it with the knowledge that God told you to do it. In the book of 1 Samuel 16:1-13, God anointed David King over Israel and he was a child at the time. David did not understand at the time of his anointing that he would have such a heavy responsibility of caring for the people of Israel. After the anointing process, David went back to taking care of the sheep. While David was taking care of the sheep, God was training him how to fight. Whenever a lion or a bear came into the area where David watched the sheep and the animal would take the sheep from the flock, David would go after the lamb and strike the lion or bear. He would deliver the lamb back into its' rightful place. (1 Samuel 17:34-35) No one can train you better than God. With this training and experience, David was very confident that he could conquer this new adversary called Goliath. Yes Goliath was bigger, mighty and stronger than David, but so were the lions and bears of David's training. It was God that gave him his courage and he did not hesitate to take on this challenge. Not only was David brave, but he was smart as well. When David found out that whoever killed Goliath would receive riches and would be exempt from taxes in Israel, he voiced his standing to kill Goliath so that he and his family would be taken care of. (1 Samuel 17:25-27) David proceeded to the Philistine giant and he used what he was familiar with. He used his sling shot and picked up five smooth stones, but it would only take one. When God anoints you and charges you to do something, no matter what it is or who you are facing, you will accomplish that task. Remember to use what God gave you. People will always voice their opinion of what they think you ought to do, but God has trained you and anointed you for the task at hand. In verse 49, David's faith was in the Lord of hosts and he was confident that he would have victory. David stood boldly so that all the earth would know that God reigned in Israel. "Then David put his hand in his bag and took out a stone; and he slung it and struck the Philistine in his forehead, so that the stone sank into his forehead, and he fell on his face to the earth." Brothers and sisters I have had my fair share of Goliaths and I'm sure I have more to fight. Please know that I, like David, was confident in the fact that in every fight that I was faced with, I knew I would win; it is promised that "we" already have the victory. You have heard the phrase, "that when you reach new levels, you will encounter new devils". This is a true statement. You need to know this is a factor. Not for you to be afraid, but to prepare you for the fight. God will anoint you for the fight. The enemy is fighting you differently from the tactical way in Joshua and David's day. The anointing can't be taught it has to be caught! You have to have the ear to hear and the heart to receive what God is preparing you for.

Your condition may be bleak and dim to you right now, but it will not stay like that. You are a child of God and He will raise you up in these trying circumstances. The anointing has been showered upon you. However, to be the leader and brave one like David, the anointing doesn't flow until it finds the right head! Stay strong and be encouraged throughout your walk with God because if you want to receive the anointing, the courage, and the strength that the people in the Bible received, you have to have the heart of the Lord and the obedience to move when He speaks to you.

Spirit of the Living God, Father I pray in the name of Jesus that you will give the reader, the listener the spirit of courage and boldness in their lives to achieve everything You set before them. I pray that they will have the valor to speak and proclaim all that You have promised to them before the beginning of this world. As your man of God, I come to the throne of God with their petitions on my lips so that others may know you in the pardon of their sins. May you pour into them the comfort and the courage of your "word" and of your "will." Father, we are the righteous in You only. We can do nothing without You. For in you Lord, we are complete, we are prosperous, we are bold as the lion in Jesus name, we pray. Amen!

Chapter 12

Longsuffering

Galatians 5:22-23

But the fruit of the Spirit is love, joy, peace, longsuffering, gentleness, goodness, faith, meekness, temperance: against such there is no law.

The fruit of the spirit amongst people today seems a little distant in our world of fellowshipping and relationships. The passion to show love to one another happens in sporadic expressions for our fellow brothers and sisters only after careful consideration. Showing love and longsuffering is on trial and era with each and every person that comes across our paths. There is suspicion first before you even get to know someone. Why has the world become hesitant to show longsuffering? To have the spirit of longsuffering enables you to forbear and forgive others even when they may not deserve forgiveness in our standards. (Colossians 3:13, "Forbearing one another, and forgiving one another, if any man have a quarrel against any: even as Christ forgave you, so also [do] you"). As with the other manifestations of the spiritual fruits, we cannot produce this fruit with in ourselves. The ability to be longsuffering comes from the Holy Spirit and by loving God's law.

We live in a time where we want microwave ministry, pop-up love, e-mailed love notes, dial-a-prayer and go. We do not want to wait for a minute for anything, if we don't have to. We look for the fastest results in banking, the fastest home that can be built to turn a profit, the quickest car coming off the assembly line. Just so we can say that we were the first to drive one. Have you ever taken a moment to think that maybe, just maybe, the reason there is so much medication today to help you fix this or that because you refuse to slow down just a little bit? Please do not get me wrong, or misunderstand me. I use the microwave sometimes as well. Modern technology has improved our lives in a way that our forefathers could not have imagined. I enjoy cooking and making different dishes, but please don't hand me a pack of minute rice. I refuse to use it. Call me old fashion, but I enjoy taking my time to prepare and create a lustrous meal that is scrumptious with every bite. When I'm finished preparing a meal, I feel that I have accomplish something worth salivating and allowing this meal to be a wonderful memory for the future. Thanksgiving and the Christmas holidays are my favorite times of the year. You won't catch me rushing a meal and using one and two minute shortcuts.

Spirit and Flesh

My cooking experiences are human and personal desires to stay in tune with the things that I really enjoy. However, there is in every one of us a struggle between the flesh and the spirit. The flesh, which is the corrupt and carnal part of us, that strives and struggles against the spirit. We have to deny our flesh daily and draw nigh to what is spiritual. On the other hand, the spirit is the supernatural part of us that comes against the flesh daily. This is where the struggle that Paul was trying to get us to understand and to prepare us for, in the struggle between spirit and flesh. Romans 7:15 says it this way, "For that which I do, I allow not: for what I would, that do I not; but what I hate, that do I". See Paul was trying to share with us the agony of trying to do the right thing, but his flesh would not cooperate with his spirit. So what happens?

Your ability to have longsuffering takes one too many hits and you start obeying your flesh. This law of spirituality and carnal flesh is also under the law of grace and mercy and the spirit that dwells in us will not suffer us to do all the evil, which our corrupt nature would prompt us to. Because this fight is a continual battle, we cannot do all the good that we would do, simply by the oppositions of our spiritual and fleshly nature either. This is why we feel conviction when we do or say something that does not resemble the longsuffering of love. Our inner natural man or woman rings an alarm in our conscience, so that our heart will strive to do the right action. With our fight to allow the spirit to control our actions, we must suppress the actions of the flesh. Understand that in the mind of the Believer, the strong principles of good will be challenged by an old habit, old friends, or even new ones. That is why this particular fruit of the spirit is called longsuffering. With God's grace on our side, it is up to us to exercise the spirit of love as long as we walk and breathe in this world. For God is my heavenly Father, please know that you are my brothers and sisters, and you better believe that the devil is no kin to us!

You have to talk back to the devil and let him know that you know who you are and you will not take his foolishness. You have to speak to that thing that is ailing you. The enemy will try to frustrate you and confusion you, just to keep your mind off of what God has purposed for you to walk out. You are a Christian and you have tried to do what God has commissioned you to do at this time and you have vowed to do your best. Do not think for one second that Satan did not hear you open your mouth and make that vow in the atmosphere. He will challenge you and test you to see how you will handle adversity. Have you ever had a business relationship with someone who made a commitment but later said, "Well, things changed, so I cannot honor our original agreement"? Sometimes this may be the case, but often it is simply an opportunity to avoid fulfilling an agreement. God is big on fulfilling vows and He expects us to honor them as well. God's nature is righteousness and truth. You will always see God honor His Word. God says there are consequences when we do not fulfill our vows. Satan knows there are consequences and presents obstacles before you, so you have to choose to do this or that. When you started out, you knew exactly what you had to do, but you did not have other options when you made the original decision to do this particular project. When we delay or make the wrong choice, God shows us longsuffering because of His love for us. So do not spend a lot of your time focusing on what you did wrong or maybe what you are going through right now. God loves you and will bring you out of whatever situation you are facing, so spend your time focusing on where God is taking you. God's going to turn your setbacks into comebacks, your pressures into power, your pains into praise, your stumbling blocks into stepping stones, your mourning into dancing, and your bruises into benedictions. Your struggles are simply opportunities for the sheer brilliance of God to be made manifest! If you continue to seek His face, God will bless you in the midst of all of your struggles!

Faithful

He is just and faithful and He calls us to wait patiently for His promises over our lives. A part of longsuffering is waiting patiently. God patiently waits for us to come to Him when we are unsure of ourselves. When we are in need, we are able to hold onto hope because we know God's character. When know that at anytime, He can change our situation around. At any moment He can answer petitioned prayers. However, the longsuffering principle does not only applies' between

God and you. We are to demonstrate this same principle with those who are much less reliable than God. 1 Thessalonians 5:14-15 says, "And we urge you, brethren, admonish the unruly, encourage the fainthearted, help the weak, be patient with all men. See that no one repays another with evil for evil, but always seek after that which is good for one another and for all men". We have to show longsuffering love to those who has hurt us, miss used are kindness and took our character as weakness. There is little to no confidence in those who have hurt us to the core of our souls. We have to find a way to let whatever someone has said to us, or have done to us go. We have to release that cancer of hate, anger, and bitterness out of our hearts and minds. So we may be able to function within the characteristic as a Christian and love others with the love of God. You have to remember that God is our Savior and our judge and there will be a day that He judges those who has transgressed against us. He will display both mercy and justice. We should not sit around and wait for that day to happen so we can gloat and smile at how God disciplines that person. We should continue to pray for them and pray that you never treat anyone in your path, with ungodly character. You want to be a light to someone else and allow him or her to see Christ in you and through you.

One of the plans and purposes for our very existence is to be an example and a light that resembles God. We must conform to His likeness and unconditionally trust Him. How many times have you put your trust in that friend who said that they would be with you through thick and thin? You found out that when things began to get thick, they bailed out on you and you were left standing alone. How many times have you put your money into the stock market, expecting a large payday some day; only to get a phone call with the news that the stock market that you invested in, crashed? Trust is earned and achieved through many different issues of life. We trust God because we have gone through enough of something to know that He is here for us and from knowing what His will is, and we literally walk it out. Trust doesn't just ''happen''; it's a learned experience. The truth in this matter is that people in this world can be very difficult to deal with or get along with. Simple put, people are not always nice. With God, we learned to trust Him because of all the mess that He has brought us out of. Some people still do not trust God because He has not acted like a genie in their life and performed some act for them when and how they wanted it. No one will lay their life on the line for someone if they don't believe that person loves them. In 1 John 4:19 it says, "We love him, because he first loved us". Since the beginning of creation, we were created in His image, in His likeliness an in His love. Because of this, He has given us an example on how to love and trust, which is already in side of you. After the fall of man, God so loved the world that He gave us His own begotten son. God loved us, even when we were both unloving and unwilling to love. God in His omnipotent power continues to love us through the fruit of the spirit, longsuffering.

It is such a blessing that God bears suffering longer than we do. He is slow to anger, but you never want to be in His wrath. The display of longsuffering is proof of God's goodness, love, faithfulness and His desire to grant us salvation. Romans 2:4 reads, "Or despisest thou the riches of his goodness and forbearance and longsuffering; not knowing that the goodness of God leadeth thee to repentance?" Forbearance is refraining from the enforcement of something that is due like a debt, a right, or an obligation. Longsuffering differs slightly in that its emphasis is on temperament. What is your temperament level? What pushes your buttons to the point of irritability or uncomfortable sensitivity levels, which causes you to forget about longsuffering? Let us talk about debt and financial situations. I want to talk about that because that is the first place where anybody can start trouble. I don't want to rub you the wrong way or get on your nerves, but use this time to check your personal, tolerable meter. We like to talk about the wealth being stored up for the righteous and the abundant harvest that is coming our way. That is true and I believe in the biblical principle in order to receive the power to get wealth. It is our responsibility to be good stewards with our possessions and money. When we are blessed with more money, we are to exercise proper discipline with our increase. In Proverbs 21:20 it says, "There is treasure to be desired and oil in the dwelling of the wise; but a foolish man spendeth it up". Some people wrestle with restraint of spending more than they make. Bills are made and when the creditor calls your house, you're upset with them because you have faulted on financially paying them back. I'm not talking about unexpected hardships that are out of your control. I'm trying to help those who frivolously spend more than they should. Don't you get tired of saying, "I'm just trying to make ends meet"? Debt puts strain on you and that is like saying that you enjoy carrying too much weight. Another scripture that you need to make yourself familiar with is Romans 13:8, "Owe no man any thing (nothing), but to love one another: for he that loveth another hath fulfilled the law". God expects us to pay our debts as well as our tithes (Malachi 3:10).

Money can fuel your best dreams or it can grow into your worst nightmares. Money issues are the main reason why couples argue, break up and if they are married, divorce. To handle money properly gives you a means of freedom. You can have freedom from financial pressures, which will help you to argue less and will allow you to allocate your money wisely. Until you develop a plan, your mate, the bill collector, and your pastor has to practice longsuffering until you begin to become more financially responsible. The sooner you can develop or get help with a development plan to strategize your financial situation, the sooner your life will change for the better. Keep in mind to have God's input in your financial plan and ask Him for help with your finances.

Dry Place

Please do not think that you do not have enough for God to work with. God wants the whole you. Not the good parts, not the ok parts, not the just enough in between to get me by parts. God is the master of longsuffering and if you think your life is too messed up for God to do anything about, examine the story of Ezekiel in the Valley of Dry Bones (Ezekiel 37:1-14). God told Ezekiel to speak His word over a dead situation. Can you imagine walking into a gloomy, dry place and looking at bones that had been decomposed for years and then asked to trust God. Trust in His word that these bones would live again. What an incredible situation for Ezekiel to be in. I'm pretty sure that Ezekiel had never seen anything like this before. God took Ezekiel told him to prophesy to the dry bones. God told Ezekiel to speak His word over them and He would put breath into them. This undoubtedly was the most impacting experience in Ezekiel's life. He was able to see for himself, a miracle from God. The bible says that there was a noise after he prophesied. Suddenly, the bones began to rattle and then they came together. Muscle began to form and tissue began to form. Eyes grew into the sockets and hair began to grow out of the follicles. My, my, my. To Ezekiel's amazement, he was looking at people now. They were not moving, but they were people. Then God had him to prophesy to the breath of life because the people were not breathing. The wind came from the four corners of the earth to fill these corpses. The Breath of Life entered into the dry bones and they came together and stood up on their feet. What a powerful story, but do you want to get back on your feet? You have been longsuffering in one area of your life that you know you could do better in. We all can improve somewhere, but we just don't take the time to start. Sometimes we listen to the voices that tell us that it is too late for us. That time has past. God has given that blessing to someone else. The devil is a liar! Begin to breathe life into your area of need and immerse yourself into God's word. Ezekiel could not have revived that dead situation with his knowledge, wisdom, money or strength. It was fulfilled only because of the power of God. Without Him there is no hope, there is nothing you could do without Him. God freely gives His life for those who have been slain by circumstances or held captive by the lies of the enemy. Seek the Lord's face and cry out to Him. Let Him know that it is you O' Lord, standing in the need of prayer.

You know, I used to think that I could only pray one way or I had to pray at a certain time. I was wrong. It was my own miss guided thinking on the scripture "pray without ceasing" (1 Thessalonians 5:17), which caused me to create shortcomings for myself. When I prayed, I could not stay on my knees all day. Thank you God for revelation. He showed me in scripture and in preaching that I could pray anywhere, at anytime. My awareness to prayer increased and I realized that I could pray in my car, I could pray at the mall, I could pray on my job, and yes, I still can pray at school. My prayer invokes His presence into my invisible sanctuary. He delights Himself in my prayer time, in my praise and worship time. Having a simple song in my heart sends the transgressions away.

In Revelation 8:1, John writes, "...there was silence in heaven for about half an hour". Why do you think there was silence? In verse 4 John explains that the prayers of the saints went up before God from the angel's hand. That is how important and powerful prayer is. God will stop to listen to your prayers and my prayers. He will consider your thoughts, dreams, struggles, fears, set backs, setups, and desires just because He loves us so much. To other people, your thoughts or concerns may not mean much to them, but God holds them dear to his heart and He will give you an answer in His time and He will move on our behalf. This is a little something that I have posted on my computer at work to encourage myself when things go wrong. "When the outlook is gloomy, just remember that the up look is glorious!"

Perseverance

This level of faith and believing in God's word did not just happen over night. There have been some longsuffering and growing pains on my part. There were days were I wanted to give up, quit, stop fighting to do good. After enough set backs in life, like loosing your job, loosing both parents, coming close to loosing my life, loosing your house, or your car, you start to wonder if you should keep on trying. The answer to that question is "Yes"! You cannot give up. Life will bring to you speed bumps, unexpected accidents, sometimes even tragedies. I have been knocked down and the wind has been knocked out of me, but I knew that I had to get up. The Armor of God is useful when I'm standing up, not when I'm staying down. In the middle of a spiritual battle, I had to listen to God's voice and remember who He said I am. Not giving weight to what others tried to make me out to be. When my heart was broken, God healed my heart and took away the pain. He took broken experiences and allowed me love others as God wants people to be loved. Relying on God's word and His strength will help anyone who is willing to give it to Jesus. I believe we have more drive and determination when we know our finish line. The bible said of Jesus that it was for the joy that was set before him that he endured the shame of the Cross. See Jesus saw us in the future, and that is why he dealt with the pain of baring the old rugged cross and endured the excruciating pain of 39 hellacious stripes on our behalf. Beloved, no matter what you are going through right now, see yourself in the future, because it looks much better than it does right now. We have to learn how to appreciate longsuffering.

God's longsuffering is seen in His gracious restraint of His wrath towards those who deserve it. Think about all the people that have done some horrible acts of hate crimes. The high school shootings, the terrorist attacks on 911 in New York, the beating and dragging of a man in Texas. This man was helplessly tied to the back of a speeding truck. The wrath of God could have easily been justified to come down and punish the perpetrators, however He saw fit. Despite the rebellious condition of the world, He waits patiently for humans to turn from their wicked ways. God's longsuffering does not overlook anything or anybody. He sees all and He knows all. Unlike man, God has the end in view. He is Alpha and Omega, the beginning and the end. He has true insight of everything that is happening. His ways are not our ways and His thoughts are not like our thoughts. God does not become persuaded by human emotions. God's remarkable patients and endurance in handling sinners demonstrates His superb longsuffering. God promises that He will be long-tempered with us and we should repent from our sinful thoughts or actions and dedicate ourselves to the obedience and service of God. To serve God's people as He admonishes us to, will develop the quality of how we should display longsuffering through serving others and resilient dedication to Him.

Temperament

Longsuffering is patience that we all must learn to embrace as we grow spiritually. Showing patience will develop your heart to be kind to others and your temper will become mild and meek. You will have a gentle spirit and with enough exercise your act of patience will become constant in all circumstances. You will have some set backs and loose your temper. God is the one who will be your fitness trainer. The real test of patience is not in waiting, but in how one acts while he or she is waiting. Our enemy knows that you want to exercise your patience and he wants you to loose your thoughts, loose your mind so he can get you to do what he wants you to do. A person who has developed patience will be able to put up with things without losing his or her temper. In James 1:4, he says it like this, *"But let patience have her perfect work, that ye may be perfect and entire, wanting (lacking) nothing."* Every opportunity that you exercise patience, the enemy goes back to the drawing board so he can figure out how to make you loose your temper. To become a Christian of unwavering patience with the stamina of a fortitude mind, you will have to practice your patient walk. To become stronger is definitely a process, which takes a lot of practice and certain situations that are designed for what you can handle. He will not put more on us than we can bear. This part of the "Fruit of the Spirit" does not seem very desirable. Who really wants to go through suffering? Not many will attest to that, but we as Christians know that it is necessary and profitable to our soul. If you are someone who is stubborn, reluctant to receive instructions and resist change every chance you get, you are setting yourself up to go through longsuffering. God has a purpose and a plan for your life and how can it affectively be walked out if you do not know how to shut your mouth. How can God use you when you treat people with disrespect? As in everything else, Jesus Christ sets the standard of longsuffering. He is the ultimate teacher and His will shall be done. Jesus was hung up for our hang-ups! With that said, you should run to Jesus every chance you get. If you mess up on this journey, and trust me you will, do not run from God, run to Him. His longsuffering and love is waiting for you. You may think that you are the only person in the world who is going through what you are going through. I am here to tell you that you are not. You are the one person in this world who can make a difference in someone else's life right around you. God teaches us and grooms us to help others. Christians sometimes forget what kind of power they have inside of them. God have made Believers in such a way that when the people of the world are sitting, the Believers are standing. When the enemy comes against us, the Lord will raise up a standard against them. God's standard is so great and glorious that His standard prepares us to be used. Psalm 9:10 says, "Those who know your name trust in you, for you, O LORD, have never abandoned anyone who searches for you." The "Fruit of the Spirit" is a gift from God and it requires love. You will have to seek the Lord and search your heart to receive the many gifts from God. Love takes precedence in this list of gifts of the "Fruit of the Spirit". Having love is an attribute, which requires you to suffer long sometimes. You can achieve complete fulfillment with the love of God dwelling and working inside of you. The longsuffering part, teaches us patience when we don't want to wait. It will teach us how to hold on to hope when things look weary. Allow your heart to be filled with love because in the book of 1 Samuel 16:7, it states that, "The Lord does not look at the things man looks at. Man looks at the outward appearance, but the Lord looks at the heart".

To my brothers and sisters in the Lord, I pray that the Lord will continue to dwell with in your heart and He shall remove all of the hurt, the fear, the doubts, and the weariness from your heart. Storms may blow and troubles may come, but the Lord is on our side and He shall fight our battles. Lord I pray that you continue to smile upon every soul that is receiving this prayer. May the meditation of your words become stitched into their hearts. Allow our trust level to become heightened with your word. May our lifestyle become a life after you Lord and allow them to be a beacon of light along this journey. I beg of your continued help that we may draw all men and women unto you. In Jesus Holy and Majestic name we pray, Amen!

Notes:

References:

The Thompson Chain-Reference Bible KJV
Fifth Improved Edition
Copyright © 1988 By the B. B. Kirkbride Bible Company, Inc.

The Open Bible - New King James Version
Copyright © 1983, 1985, 1990, 1997 By Thomas Nelson, Inc.

The Holy bible, New King James Version
Copyright © 1982 by Thomas Nelson, Inc.

Helen Keller reference
http://www.rnib.org.uk/xpedio/groups/public/documents/publicwebsite/public_keller.hcsp#P8_883
Copyright © 1995-2007 Royal National Institute of the Blind, Registered Charity Number 226227

Thomas Edison reference
http://www.thomasedison.com/biog.htm
By Gerald Beals Copyright © 1999 All Rights Reserved

About the Author

Minister Johnnie B. Sanders, Jr.

Preacher, Teacher, Counselor, and Educator; These are just but a few of the words to describe the dynamic and life changing ministry of Minister Johnnie B. Sanders. For over three decades Minister Sanders has honed and shaped a lifetime of strong character, integrity, and morality in to a ministry that is poised to change the lives of the body of Christ.

Since the early 80's Minister Sanders has devoted his life to seeing the transforming power of Jesus operate in the lives of people in every culture crossing social and economic divides. From his work with the FCA (Fellowship of Christian Athletes), the creation and organization of In Home Bible Fellowship, Community Ministry that provided food, clothing, lights, air conditioning and repairs to homes, to music ministry in the local church, Minister Sanders focus has always been on service.

Now Minister Johnnie B. Sanders stands ready to take the spirit of servitude to the next level. Upon completing his ministerial training at The Potters House School of Ministry in Dallas under the auspices of Bishop T.D. Jakes in 2001, he quickly enrolled at Dallas Baptist University and received a Bachelor of Arts and Sciences degree, with a major in Management Information Systems. He also did educational studies emphasizing in psychology, sociology, and counseling in 2003. Minister Sanders was called upon to serve as Chaplain during his enrollment at DBU. He has also received certification in Christian Counseling from the American Association of Christian Counselors in 2004.

With his years of experience and heart to empower his community, Minister Sanders now continues his work as an influential radio personality by co-hosting a talk show on Heaven 97 KHVN. A true trailblazer in the work of an evangelist, in 2006 Minister Sanders became host of "REAL TALK with J.B. Sanders", a powerful and engaging new program via Internet television. As he continues to push the envelope to reach the masses with the message of hope, the sky is literally the limit to his many gifts and talents.

JB Sanders Ministries was launched to help facilitate the growing demand of local and national opportunities of ministry and continues to grow influentially to the surrounding communities in Dallas/Ft. Worth.

Minister Johnnie B. Sanders is proudly married to his wonderful and anointed wife, Mrs. Marcene Sanders, and they reside in the beautiful suburb of Valley Ranch, TX.

Printed in the United States
105557LV00005B/52-60/A

9 781434 315199